Life in the Real World

5-Minute Devotions for Teens

Eileen Ritter

CPH
SAINT LOUIS

Copyright © 1997 Concordia Publishing House
3558 S. Jefferson Avenue, St. Louis, MO 63118-3968
Manufactured in the United States of America

Library of Congress Cataloging-in-Publication Data

Ritter, Eileen, 1943-
    Life in the real world: 5-minute devotions for teens/Eileen Ritter.
        p. cm.
    Summary: A collection of meditations with scripture references, practical
applications, and prayers, focusing on such real-life issuses as friends and family, dating, prejudice, anger, rules, and faith.
    ISBN 0-570-04888-5
    1. Teenagers—Prayer-books and devotions—English. 2. Christian life—
Juvenile literature. [1. Prayer books and devotions. 2. Christian life.] I. Title.
BV4850.R57 1997
242'.63—dc21   96-39219
                                                         CIP
                                                          AC

    2   3   4   5   6   7   8   9   10   06   05   04   03   02   01   00   99   98   97

Contents

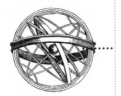

The first thing Andrew did was to find his brother Simon and tell him, "We have found the Messiah" (that is, the Christ). And he brought him to Jesus. *John 1:41–42*

Into the Word

John the Baptist—he was the preacher Andrew and his friend had set out to follow. But one day John had pointed to someone passing by and said, "Look, the Lamb of God." So Andrew and his friend followed Jesus.

They followed; they listened; they spent the rest of the day with Jesus. By evening Andrew realized that this Teacher was the Christ, the promised Messiah.

Overwhelmed by this discovery, what did Andrew do? He didn't write a book of the Bible or establish half a dozen churches in Asia. Ordinary Andrew went home and told his brother, his partner in the family fishing business. And he brought his brother to Jesus.

Jesus recognized Andrew's brother and greeted him by name: "You are Simon son of John. You will be called Cephas" (which, when translated, is Peter) (John 1:42). Peter—who walked on the water and witnessed the transfiguration, who confessed Jesus as the Son of the living God and later denied Him in the high priest's courtyard, who was forgiven and then commissioned to feed the Savior's sheep and lambs. Peter preached to thousands in Jerusalem, led the early Christian church, and died a martyr's death in Rome. Peter, by the power of the Holy Spirit, turned the first-century world upside-down for Jesus.

Something to Think About

Andrew lived his ordinary life in the shadow of his impulsive, colorful brother, Peter. Think about a time when you have felt ordinary compared to a brother or sister or friend.

Andrew, like the other disciples, was commissioned by Jesus to "Go and make disciples of all nations" (Matthew 28:19). But his most important convert was his brother, Simon Peter. Name in your heart someone in your home or in your immediate circle of friends whom you could ask the Holy Spirit to help you bring to Jesus. Think of two or three ways you could begin.

Prayer

Lord Jesus, like Andrew I know You are the Messiah, the One God sent to be my Savior. Like Andrew I want to bring my brother (sister, friend), _____, to You. Show me, through Your Holy Spirit, what to do and say. Amen.

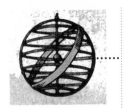

Jesus said to the servants, "Fill the jars with water;" so they filled them to the brim. Then He told them, "Now draw some out and take it to the master of the banquet." They did so, and the master of the banquet tasted the water that had been turned into wine. ... This, the first of His miraculous signs, Jesus performed in Cana of Galilee. He thus revealed His glory, and His disciples put their faith in Him. *John 2:7–9, 11*

Something to Think About

The natural world generally follows ordered patterns. But sometimes—the tornado's funnel splits just as it approaches the farmhouse, the rising floodwaters stop short of the door of the church, a changing wind blows the forest fire away from the little community that stood directly in its path.

Luck—or miracle? Does God, who created the natural world, still hold power over it? Does He ever exercise that power on behalf of His people?

Into the Word

The natural order of things seemed to hold that day. Too few jugs of wine divided by too many thirsty guests equaled a hospitality nightmare for the host of the wedding banquet. An embarrassed bride and groom, a prematurely ended feast—the logical consequences of a short supply of wine.

Mary heard about it from the servants. She took her concerns to Jesus. He instructed the servants to fill six stone jars with water. Then He told them to take some of the water to the master of the banquet.

Jesus, God made Man, had shared in the work of creation, separating light from darkness and gathering the waters of the planet into seas. Now, because He loved people and cared about their needs, He changed 180 gallons of that water into wine.

Very few people at the feast—a few servants, Mary, the disciples—knew what Jesus had done. But Jesus had revealed His glory, and the Spirit increased the faith His disciples had in Him.

In My Life

Jesus is still the Lord of creation and sometimes He lets us see His glory by observing His control over nature. The next time you think you've experienced a lucky break in weather or another natural phenomenon, look for the hand of God at work.

Prayer

The world You created, Lord, is awesome and wonderful. Forgive me for often ignoring Your glory, and help me to see Your hand still at work in the forces of nature. Then let the glory all be Yours. In Jesus' name I pray. Amen.

After six days Jesus took Peter, James, and John with Him and led them up a high mountain, where they were all alone. There He was transfigured before them. *Mark 9:2*

10

Something to Think About

Mountaintop experiences—times when you've felt on top of the world. We've all enjoyed them. Maybe a coach or teacher praised your work or used it as an example of how the job should be done. Perhaps you received an award you had worked for ages to get. Maybe your family had a special time together when you felt especially loved and appreciated.

You've experienced mountaintops in your faith life too. They began when God's Holy Spirit worked faith in you at your Baptism. One may have occurred when you were confirmed and declared your faith in front of your family and the members of your congregation. Many young people experience a high like this when they first receive the Lord's Supper. Other mountaintops take place at youth gatherings or retreats or camp.

When we enjoy mountaintop experiences, we would love to make them last forever. But the reality is that all too soon life goes back to normal, with all of its plains and valleys. Only the memory of the mountaintop remains.

Into the Word

Jesus took Peter, James, and John to the mountaintop. The high they experienced was due to more than altitude. Here they saw Him confer with Moses and Elijah. Jesus' clothes were dazzling white, and they heard God the Father call Him "My Son, whom I love" (Mark 9:7). As you might expect, Peter, James, and John wanted to build three shelters and stay on the mountain forever.

But Jesus led them back down to reality, to the plains of everyday existence. Ahead lay the valley of the Kidron brook and the garden where they would fall asleep while Jesus prayed and where He would be betrayed by one of His own disciples. Ahead lay the other mountaintop, where on a cross He would die for my sins and yours and for the sins of all people.

In My Life

Mountaintop experiences come and go, to live only in memory. But Calvary's mountaintop and what happened there changes your life. Through Baptism, Jesus' crucifixion becomes our own. His death to sin is ours, and His resurrection, and His life forever. "We were therefore buried with Him through baptism into death in order that, just as Christ was raised from the dead through the glory of the Father, we too may lead a new life" (Romans 6:4).

Prayer

Jesus, because of what You did on Calvary, my sins are forgiven. Help me to live a new life for You. Amen.

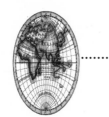

During the fourth watch of the night Jesus went out to them, walking on the lake.

"Lord, if it's You," Peter replied, "tell me to come to You on the water."

"Come," He said.

Then Peter got down out of the boat, walked on the water and came toward Jesus. But when he saw the wind, he was afraid and, beginning to sink, cried out, "Lord, save me!"

Immediately Jesus reached out His hand and caught him. "You of little faith," He said, "why did you doubt?" *Matthew 14:25, 28–31*

Something to Think About

Of course you knew it wouldn't be easy. But you were so confident of God's help and direction, so full of enthusiasm to follow Him and lead the life He planned for you that you knew you couldn't fail. And so you stepped boldly out of the boat ...

You entered a new school year, resolving this time to do your best, to be the person God intended you to be—to complete the assigned homework every night, to pay attention in class, to participate in group discussions, to run for student government, and to make a difference in your school community. But before the end of September waves of laziness and indifference caused you to begin to sink in piles of incomplete assignments and missed deadlines.

You resolved to keep yourself sexually pure, as God intends. You would respect the body He gave you and made His own temple. And you would treat others with respect and responsibility too. But the sexually explicit images of movies and TV and pop music and your own hormones roar like waves, tempting you away from your God-pleasing intentions.

You renewed your baptismal vow at your confirmation, promising to be faithful to Jesus until death. You delighted in receiving His body and blood in the Sacrament. You worshiped joyfully. But the undertow of activities and friends tries to pull you away from your Lord.

Into the Word

Like you, Peter stepped boldly out of the boat. With strong faith he walked toward Jesus. With eyes fixed on Jesus, he could not fail. Only when the waves distracted him from Jesus did he begin to sink. His focus on his own inadequacies and troubles marked his doom. But Jesus' outstretched hand saved him.

Prayer Thought

Do you hear the waves rolling close to you? Ask Jesus to keep your eyes focused on Him in the midst of all the difficult circumstances around you.

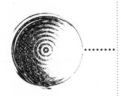

Then seizing Him, they led Him away and took Him into the house of the high priest. Peter followed at a distance. But when they had kindled a fire in the middle of the courtyard and had sat down together, Peter sat down with them. A servant girl saw him seated there in the firelight. She looked closely at him and said, "This man was with Him."

But he denied it. "Woman, I don't know Him," he said. *Luke 22:54–57*

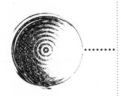

In My Life

You close your locker and start down the hall. There, in front of the main office, they seem to be waiting for you. Three of the guys from the football team. The cheerleader with the curly blond hair and the pretty smile. The student council president. The five most popular kids in school, none of whom have ever acknowledged you're alive.

The cheerleader smiles a welcoming smile, and one of the jocks looks like he's ready to start a conversation. You can't believe your good fortune. And then the maroon fabric of your sweatshirt sleeve catches your eye, and you remember what you're wearing. Your youth group shirt—the one with the cross and the Bible verse right there on the front. Of all the clothes you could have worn today, it would have to be that shirt.

Into the Word

Peter knew that feeling. The evening had been so confusing: His Master, Jesus, washing his feet as a servant would do; all that talk about one of the gang betraying Jesus; trying to stay awake while Jesus prayed in the garden; then the temple guard, led by his friend Judas, arresting Jesus and hauling Him off to the high priest's palace.

Now Peter stood in the palace courtyard. He inched toward the soldiers around the fire. How safe it would be to join their little circle, to be a part of the "in" crowd. How frightening to be reminded of his association with Jesus. How much easier to deny Him.

Jesus understood Peter's fears. After His death and resurrection He assured Peter of His love and forgiveness. He included Peter in the work of building His kingdom. And He understands, assures, forgives, and includes you too.

Prayer Thought

Read 1 Peter 3:15. Then ask Jesus to help you to trust Him and to be ready to give an account of your faith.

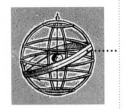

When a Samaritan woman came to draw water, Jesus said to her, "Will you give Me a drink?" (His disciples had gone into the town to buy food.)

The Samaritan woman said to Him, "You are a Jew and I am a Samaritan woman. How can You ask me for a drink?" (For Jews do not associate with Samaritans.)

Jesus answered her, "If you knew the gift of God and who it is that asks you for a drink, you would have asked Him and He would have given you living water." *John 4:7-10*

In My Life

We want so much to believe it's a thing of the past, something we read about in American history in the unit leading up to civil rights. Jim Crow laws. Lynchings. Cross burnings by midnight riders in white hoods. Segregated schools. Prejudice.

Haven't we just traded blatant racism for more subtle forms? Our classrooms are integrated, but teachers may have different expectations of students from different ethnic backgrounds. African-American students are stereotyped as basketball players or members of the Glee Club (singing spirituals, of course), never as members of the chess club or debate club or Science Olympiad. We're not prejudiced, of course—it's just that none of "them" happen to be part of our circle of friends.

Think about your own school. Can you remember three examples of racial prejudice that you have seen?

Into the Word

Jews of Jesus' day hated traveling through

Samaria. Their half-breed cousins, the Samaritans, didn't follow the Jewish religion completely, worshiping on Mt. Gerizim instead of in Jerusalem. Jews avoided contact with Samaritans whenever possible.

Jesus, a Jewish rabbi, met a Samaritan woman at a well. This woman's reputation was well known because she had had five husbands and was now living in a state of adultery. Most Jewish rabbis would have denounced and avoided her; even the most liberal would not have included her in their circle of friends.

But Jesus asked her for a drink. And He offered her the one thing she needed most—living water, which would become a perpetual spring within her, renewing her with eternal life. The same living water He offers to you and me in Baptism.

When prejudice raises its ugly head in your school or your world, remember Jesus and the Samaritan woman. Ask God's Spirit to renew you with His living water, and follow the example of the One who died to free you to love others.

Prayer

Lord Jesus, forgive me for judging others because of color or ethnic background. Help me to love others as You have loved me. Amen.

Blessed is the man who does not walk in the counsel of the wicked or stand in the way of sinners or sit in the seat of mockers. But his delight is in the law of the LORD, and on His law he meditates day and night.
Psalm 1:1–2

Something to Think About

Katie had looked forward to going to the big, public junior high school for months. But now that school had started, she was so nervous she could hardly function.

Classes weren't so bad. At least in class most of the attention was focused on the teacher, and people forgot that she was new and didn't have any friends. But at lunch—Katie would never forget the humiliation of sitting all alone in that noisy lunchroom where everyone else had friends.

As the weeks passed, Katie began to make new friends. First there was Blair, who rode Katie's bus home. Katie wondered why Blair missed so much school until the day Blair invited her to skip afternoon classes and to hang out at the mall.

Then came Bridget. Katie had tried to get Bridget out of the rest room before the class bell rang, but Bridget needed another minute to finish that forbidden cigarette. The assistant principal who came in to check the rest room smelled smoke on Katie as well as on Bridget and gave them both detention for the rest of the week.

And what about Amy, Steve, and Scott? They had been talking all week about the party they were going to have Saturday night. When Katie told Amy that her parents were going out of town for the weekend, the party suddenly moved to Katie's house. Katie knew her parents would never allow such a party, but she didn't want to disappoint her new friends.

Have you ever had friends like these? How did their friendship influence you?

Into the Word

The writer of Psalm 1 warns us about the influence of friends with sinful ways who give evil advice and make fun of God. He contrasts these bad friends with good friends who delight in doing what God wants them to do and who think about ways to follow Him more closely. Bad friends keep us from our walk with God; good friends encourage and support us.

Reach out to your friends through the power of the Spirit, as Jesus would, with the good news that He loves them and is their Savior too. But be careful not to let their influence pull you away from Him.

Prayer Thought

If you have had friends who have been a negative influence in your life, ask God to help you find Christian friends. Then ask Him to help you to be a Christian friend to someone else.

If an enemy were insulting me, I could endure it; if a foe were raising himself against me, I could hide from him. But it is you, a man like myself, my companion, my close friend, with whom I once enjoyed sweet fellowship as we walked with the throng at the house of God.
Psalm 55:12-14

Something to Think About

"I just couldn't believe it," Jennifer confided to her youth group counselor. "Kayla's been my best friend since second grade. We did everything together and shared all our secrets. How could she tell Kristin those lies about Greg and me?"

Jennifer had just discovered one of the differences between friends and enemies. Because you love and trust them, friends who are disloyal can hurt you much worse than enemies.

In lying about Jennifer, Kayla didn't act like a real friend. "A friend loves at all times," according to Proverbs 17:17. A real friend stands by you in times of trouble, encourages and supports you when you are weak, and rejoices with you when you are strong.

Sometimes a friend confronts you when what you are doing is wrong. But a real friend confronts and corrects in love, always helping you to live in God's way.

"Greater love has no one than this," said Jesus, "that he lay down his life for his friends" (John 15:13). Jesus, our best Friend, encourages and supports us every day in our walk with God. He comforts us when we are sad and strengthens us when we are weak. He willingly gave His own life on the cross so that we would not suffer eternal death for our sin.

In My Life

Think about the friends that God has given you. List three ways in which you could be a better friend to each of them. Then put at least one of these ideas into practice this week.

Prayer

Heavenly Father, thank You for the friends You have given me. I have not always acted like a real friend to others. Forgive me, and help me to forgive others, for the sake of my best Friend, Jesus, Your Son and my Savior. Amen.

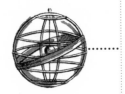

Then Jesus went around teaching from village to village. Calling the Twelve to Him, He sent them out two by two and gave them authority over evil spirits. *Mark 6:6b–7*

Into the Word

James had John, Peter had Andrew, Aquila had Priscilla, Paul had Barnabas and John, Mark and Silas. Have you noticed how often God sent teams to do His work?

In chapter 7 of his gospel, Mark records how Jesus sent His 12 disciples out among the villages to teach. Instead of sending each of them alone, He divided them into six teams of two. He could have reached more villages with 12 individuals. But Jesus knew His disciples well. He knew they would be discouraged when their listeners rejected the news they brought. He knew they would need the encouragement of their partners in ministry.

In My Life

Jesus has commissioned you for ministry in His kingdom too. "Therefore go and make disciples of all nations, baptizing them in the name of the Father and of the Son and of the Holy Spirit, and teaching them to obey everything I have commanded you" (Matthew 28:19–20). He knows that you also may become discouraged if you try to do the job alone. That's why He followed the Great Commission with the Great Promise—"And surely I am with you always, to the very end of the age" (Matthew 28:20).

Jesus provides human partners for our ministry too. Look carefully at your friends at school and in your church youth group. Is there someone with whom you can talk about your faith in Jesus and your walk with Him? Someone you can count on to support you when you stand up for your beliefs in the face of possible ridicule? This person may be one of the partners God has given you for your ministry team, to join you in the exciting task of sharing God's love with others.

Look too for opportunities to support and encourage your friends in their Christian living and witnessing. You may be one of the ministry partners God has provided for them.

Prayer

Thank You, Lord Jesus, for the privilege of witnessing for You. I know that I cannot do this alone, but You have promised to be with me. Send me Christian friends to help me in this important work, and through Your Holy Spirit help us to share Your love with others. Amen.

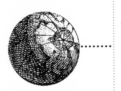

But I tell you who hear Me: Love your enemies, do good to those who hate you, bless those who curse you, pray for those who mistreat you ... Do to others as you would have them do to you. *Luke 6:27–28, 31*

In My Life

Dear God,

I need to talk to You about loving other people. Some of the things You say about it in Your Word confuse me.

I get along really well with my friends. Most of the time. And it's no wonder. I can count on them to always be there for me. When I'm happy, they're ready to celebrate with me. When I'm down, they know exactly what to say to make me feel better. They even know when it's better to say nothing at all.

It's not surprising that I love my friends, Lord. They treat me the way I want to be treated. Of course I love them in return.

But I certainly don't feel that way about my enemies.

For instance, Jim. He's made trouble for me ever since my family moved here—making fun of the way I talk, always waiting for me to make a mistake so he can point it out to everyone. Hating Jim comes naturally, but loving him? It would take a super-human *effort, Lord. I'm not sure I could do it.*

Or, Rita and Laurie and those other popular kids they're always with at school. I wanted so much to be a part of their crowd, but they never include me. Now Kim told me she heard a bad rumor about me at school, and I'm sure they're the ones who started it. How could I love people like that, Lord?

What about the drunk driver who killed my sister? When I close my eyes, I still see his face. After what he did, Lord, it would kill me to love him.

Love like You're talking about needs more than words. People ridiculed You, Lord. Your friend Judas betrayed You; Peter denied You; and Your other disciples ran away when You needed them most. A Roman governor condemned You, and foreign soldiers nailed You to the cross.

It would have been so easy to hate them, Lord. But You loved and forgave Your enemies who put You to death. Exactly the way You love and forgive me.

Help me, Lord, to love and forgive as You do. Amen.

Prayer

Forgive me, Lord, for hating people who have not loved me. Help me to love others, both friends and enemies, with a love like Yours. Amen.

Sing for joy to God our strength; shout aloud to the God of Jacob! Begin the music, strike the tambourine, play the melodious harp and lyre. Sound the ram's horn at the New Moon, and when the moon is full, on the day of our Feast; this is a decree for Israel, an ordinance of the God of Jacob. He established it as a statute for Joseph when he went out against Egypt, where we heard a language we did not understand. *Psalm 81:1–5*

Into the Word

In the Law that God gave to the people of Israel as they journeyed from Egypt to Canaan, He commanded them to observe a series of feasts and sacred days. These included Sabbath and the Sabbath Year, the Year of Jubilee, Passover, the Feast of Unleavened Bread, Firstfruits, the Festival of Weeks (Harvest or Pentecost), Trumpets (later celebrated as Rosh Hashanah or New Year's Day), Day of Atonement (Yom Kippur), Feast of Tabernacles, and Sacred Assembly. Each of these holidays commemorated something God had done: Sabbath, for example, reminded the Israelites of God's rest after creation; Passover commemorated His delivering them from slavery in Egypt and leading them to a new home.

The writer of Psalm 81 is probably talking about the Feast of Tabernacles. This seven-day, autumn festival began on the 15th day of the month (the full moon), following the Day of Atonement. This feast celebrated God's care for His people during their journey to Canaan and thanked Him for the harvest. In the annual celebration of Tabernacles, the people were reminded of what God had done for them and they praised Him for His care.

In My Life

Many of the holidays we celebrate today began as religious festivals. But holiday traditions have changed over the years, and today many "Christian" holidays have become mere secular, commercialized observances.

Think about the way your family celebrates Advent, Christmas, Lent, Easter, and Thanksgiving. Then discuss the following questions with another member of your family:

What has God done for us that we celebrate with this holiday (or season)?

What family traditions do we observe that help us remember what God has done? Which of our traditions interfere? What new ideas could we try to help us celebrate more effectively?

Prayer

Heavenly Father, You have given me special days and seasons to recall Your wonderful deeds. I am sorry that I have often left You out of my holiday celebrations. Help me to praise You every day, and especially on holidays, for all You have done for me and for saving me through Your Son, Jesus. Amen.

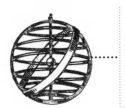

The righteous will flourish like a palm tree, they will grow like a cedar of Lebanon; planted in the house of the LORD, they will flourish in the courts of our God. They will still bear fruit in old age, they will stay fresh and green, proclaiming, "The LORD is upright; He is my Rock, and there is no wickedness in Him." *Psalm 92:12–14*

Something to Think About

It may have been different in Bible times (or even when our grandparents were children). The elders of the family or community occupied a position of respect. They were expected to give advice from the treasury of wisdom they had accumulated during their lives, and their advice was appreciated and followed.

But today the generations have flip-flopped. Styles and trends in clothing, music, slang, and leisure-time activities are set by the very young, primarily those in their teens or early twenties. Soaring sales of hair coloring, wrinkle creams, and the popularity of facelifts attest to society's attempt to stay forever young. And the elderly are ignored, rejected, and expected to keep their opinions to themselves.

Into the Word

That contrasts with the picture the psalmist gives of the elderly who, having been planted in the house of the LORD,...will flourish in the courts of our God. And not just flourish, but bear fruit—leadership for the church, advice and counsel for those still in the early stages of the journey, prayer for the people of God, and praise for the God who has sustained them throughout their lives.

In My Life

Choose an elderly person you know and with whom you feel comfortable. You may choose a grandparent, a great-aunt, or an uncle. Or, you may decide on an older man or woman from your church. Keep in mind the psalmist's description: "planted in the house of the LORD."

Visit the elderly person you have chosen. Spend time listening and really get acquainted. Then ask your elderly friend or relative to tell you about some of his or her life experiences with the Lord. What you learn may challenge your faith and inspire you in your walk with Jesus Christ.

Prayer

Thank You, Lord Jesus, for the wisdom of the older Christians in my life. Forgive me for not always taking the time to listen to them and to show them Your love. Help me to grow from the experiences they share, that we may flourish together in Your courts. Amen.

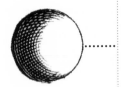

Unless the LORD builds the house, its builders labor in vain. Unless the LORD watches over the city, the watchmen stand guard in vain. In vain you rise early and stay up late, toiling for food to eat—for He grants sleep to those He loves. *Psalm 127:1-2*

Into the Word

In vain—in vain—in vain. Three times in the first two verses of Psalm 127 the psalmist tells us that our efforts will be in vain without God—building a house, the dwelling for the family; guarding the city, the center of power and security; toiling for food, providing the necessities of life.

But when the Lord builds the house—guards the city—provides the necessities—those He loves and has redeemed may rest in the quiet peace He provides.

It's all a matter of priorities, isn't it? When we rely on our own efforts, our work is in vain. When we put God first in our lives and trust in Him, He blesses us. When we try to work out our salvation and please God with our behavior, even our best efforts fail. But when we receive by faith the salvation that Jesus won for us, God counts us completely righteous for the sake of His Son.

It's like the sign on the display board outside the church: "The main thing is to keep the main thing the main thing."

Something to Think About

When God is your number one priority—when He builds the house—every aspect of your life is affected. Read each of the sentence starters below. Then finish them on paper or in your mind. You may wish to do this activity with another family member.

If God builds our house (rules our family with His Gospel love), our family relationships will ...

If God watches over our city (protects us from physical and spiritual danger), we will ...

If we trust God to provide all we need, our approach to our work will change by ...

If God is in control of our lives, we will use our money—our time—our talents ...

Prayer

On my own, Lord, my best efforts are never enough—in my family, my community, my work, or my relationship with You. Forgive me for putting myself first. Help me always to put You first in my life. In Jesus' name I pray. Amen.

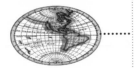

Do not suppose that I have come to bring peace to the earth. I did not come to bring peace, but a sword. For I have come to turn "a man against his father, a daughter against her mother, a daughter-in-law against her mother-in-law—a man's enemies will be the members of his own household." Anyone who loves his father or mother more than Me is not worthy of Me; anyone who loves his son or daughter more than Me is not worthy of Me; and anyone who does not take his cross and follow Me is not worthy of Me. Whoever finds his life will lose it, and whoever loses his life for My sake will find it. *Matthew 10:34–39*

Into the Word

Jesus' words in Matthew 10 seem to be in conflict with Paul's instructions in Ephesians 6:1–3: Children, obey your parents in the Lord, for this is right. "Honor your father and mother"—which is the first commandment with a promise—"that it may go well with you and that you may enjoy long life on the earth."

How can you reconcile these two texts if you live with parents who don't understand and who ridicule your faith in Jesus?

In My Life

It's hard enough to live your Christian faith when your friends make fun of you. Ridicule from parents or other family members because of your belief in Jesus hurts more. How can a young Christian remain true to his faith without dishonoring his parents when they don't share his beliefs?

First, live in obedience to your parents as the Bible commands. Causing unnecessary friction will only make it harder for them to see the difference being a Christian has made in your life.

Second, remember that it isn't your responsibility to make your parents believe in Jesus. That's the Holy Spirit's job. But it is your job to be God's representative in your home, living out the love of Christ to the members of your family, forgiving, encouraging, witnessing through the help of the Holy Spirit with your actions to your joy in being a redeemed child of God.

Third, keep God in the number one place in your life. Give Him first priority, and everything else will fall into its own place.

Last, look for Christian friends who will be there to pray for you and to support you as you live a Christian life in a difficult situation. And don't forget your best Friend to whom you can always go in prayer.

Prayer

Lord Jesus, You are my Savior from sin, my hope for eternal life. Through the Holy Spirit help me grow stronger in my faith despite the unbelief of those closest to me and help me to share You with the members of my family. Amen.

There was also a prophetess, Anna, the daughter of Phanuel, of the tribe of Asher. She was very old; she had lived with her husband seven years after her marriage, and then was a widow until she was eighty-four. She never left the temple but worshiped night and day, fasting and praying. Coming up to them at that very moment, she gave thanks to God and spoke about the Child to all who were looking forward to the redemption of Jerusalem. *Luke 2:36–38*

Into the Word

Old people. What do they know? Born before computers and space flights, genetic engineering and the information superhighway, what could they possibly know that could affect our lives?

Luke tells us about two fascinating old people in the second chapter of his gospel. Anna, an 84-year-old widow, stayed in the temple day and night fasting and praying. Luke describes her as a prophetess; coming up to Mary and Joseph and the infant Jesus, she gave thanks to God and spoke about the Child to all who were looking forward to the redemption of Jerusalem.

Just before this text Luke tells about Simeon, a devout and righteous man who had been waiting for years to see the Messiah God had promised to send to Israel. In fact, the Holy Spirit had promised Simeon that he would not die until he had seen the Promised One. On the day Mary and Joseph brought Jesus to the temple, the Holy Spirit inspired Simeon to go to the temple to meet them. "Sovereign Lord, as You have promised, You now dismiss Your servant in peace," Simeon praised God. "For my eyes have seen Your salvation, which You have prepared in the sight of all people, a light for revelation to the Gentiles and for glory to Your people Israel" (Luke 2:29–32).

Something to Think About

Think about the older people in your life. Do your grandparents seem to be out of touch with modern reality? Does the older generation at church live in the past and grumble about the present?

The clearest insight into what was happening that day in the temple in Jerusalem was in the age-clouded eyes of Simeon and Anna. Because of their faithfulness, God gave them a clear view of His Son whom He had sent to be their Savior. In faith they recognized Jesus as the fulfillment of Old Testament prophecy and as the hope of salvation for people of all nations.

Look again at the older people in your family and in your church. Listen to their advice. Learn from their experiences. Share their faith.

Prayer Thought

Praise God for the older saints He has given you for examples.

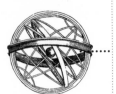

The son said to him, "Father, I have sinned against heaven and against you. I am no longer worthy to be called your son."

But the father said to his servants, "... For this son of mine was dead and is alive again; he was lost and is found." *Luke 15:21–22, 23*

Something to Think About

Turn on the morning talk shows on TV and you'll find at least one "lost son" or "lost daughter" every day. "Teenagers Whose Parents Have Thrown Them Out of the House." "Girls Who Get Pregnant to Hurt Their Parents." "Teenaged Boys Arrested for Physically Abusing Their Mothers and Fathers." "Fights with My Parents Forced Me to Join a Gang." The host addresses questions to a panel of middle-aged bigots sitting beside surly, pouting adolescents. Hate-filled responses contain more bleeps than words.

In My Life

To an outsider, your fights with your parents may seem mild by comparison. But to you (and to your parents) they cause stress and pain. Left unresolved, anger leads to hate, hurt feelings to resentment, suspicion, and mistrust.

Think of the last three unresolved arguments you had with your parents. Who was responsible? If you answered honestly, you probably had to admit that you at least shared in the responsibility. And you probably shared in that miserable, guilty feeling that hung on in the silence after the storm.

What would it take to resolve those three arguments and restore the relationship God intended for your family? You may be surprised to discover it will take only five words, but they're the hardest words in the English language to say. Although you would like to hear your parents say these words, the only person you can make say them is you, yourself. Try them on your parents and see what happens.

"I was wrong. I'm sorry."

Into the Word

The Prodigal Son in the story Jesus told said them. And his father killed the fatted calf and threw a barbecue. His father forgave him. And the relationship was restored.

Jesus told the story to show us how our heavenly Father forgives us and welcomes us home when we confess our sins to Him and tell Him we are sorry. And human parents, especially those who share with us our faith in God's love and forgiveness, try to forgive and welcome us home the same way.

Prayer

Heavenly Father, I have sinned against You and against my parents. I trust in Your forgiveness because I believe that Jesus died to pay for my sins. Help me to ask for and to receive the forgiveness of my human parents too. For Jesus' sake. Amen.

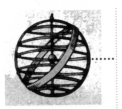

God is our refuge and strength, an ever-present help in trouble. Therefore we will not fear, though the earth give way and the mountains fall into the heart of the sea, though its waters roar and foam and the mountains quake with their surging. *Psalm 46:1–3*

Something to Think About

Since the first atomic bombs were dropped on Hiroshima and Nagasaki in 1945, the possibility of cities and mountains crumbling from the destruction of nuclear holocaust has never been far from our minds. The potential devastation of such a disaster rivals the opening verses of Psalm 46: the earth giving way, mountains falling into the sea, the ocean itself in upheaval.

Living in our modern age means knowing constant, paralyzing fear. Was it any different for the psalmist?

What are your five greatest fears?

Into the Word

St. John, who was once the disciple of Jesus, used similar phrases to describe the last days of the earth: "There was a great earthquake. The sun turned black like sackcloth made of goat hair, the whole moon turned blood red, and the stars in the sky fell to earth, ... and every mountain and island was removed from its place" (Revelation 6:12–14). For fear of facing God's judgment, sinful people called to the mountains to fall on them and hide them from God the Judge.

In My Life

The psalmist pointed out the one place of safety in the midst of all this devastation: "God is our refuge and strength, an ever-present help in trouble" (Psalm 46:1). Because He is with us, we have no reason to fear. Not natural disasters. Not man-made weapons of destruction. Not even the coming Day of Judgment. For on that day the Judge of all will see us clothed in the righteousness of His Son, Jesus, and take us to heaven to be with Him forever.

St. Paul, contemplating on all the terrors of his world and ours, described God, our Refuge, like this: "For I am convinced that neither death nor life, neither angels nor demons, neither the present nor the future, nor any powers, neither height nor depth, nor anything else in all creation, will be able to separate us from the love of God that is in Christ Jesus our Lord" (Romans 8:38–39).

Prayer

God, You are my refuge and strength, and nothing can separate me from Your love. Keep me safe in Your care, and help me to trust You and not be afraid. Amen.

Surely he will never be shaken; a righteous man will be remembered forever. He will have no fear of bad news; his heart is steadfast, trusting in the LORD. His heart is secure, he will have no fear; in the end he will look in triumph on his foes. Psalm 112:6–8

Something to Think About

Who was your hero when you were a child? Wonder Woman? Superman or Batman? A truck or race car that transformed itself into a robot? A turtle who dressed like a ninja warrior and practiced karate?

No matter which superhero you idolized, it's safe to guess one of your hero's most impressive characteristics—absolute fearlessness. That's why little children, who are afraid of everything from monsters under the bed to big kids at the bus stop, love them so.

Think about your favorite hero. How did he or she show fearlessness in the face of characters or forces that would have frightened you?

Into the Word

One kind of fear, however, is good. We read in Proverbs 1:7 that "the fear of the LORD is the beginning of knowledge." This kind of fear means a loving respect or reverence for God, obeying Him as Lord, and trusting in His promises. We recognize that God is omnipotent, more powerful than any of the characters or forces that frighten us.

When we completely trust our all-powerful God to take care of us, all of our fears subside. Surely God the Creator can protect us from storms and floods, from earthquakes and other natural disasters. These are, after all, a part of the natural order He established. Neither do we need to fear what people can do to us; the Lord of life and death has control over all that happens to His children.

God has even defeated our greatest enemies of all—sin, death, and the devil himself. He accomplished this by sending His own Son, Jesus, to suffer and die in our place for our sins. God holds His redeemed children safely in His hand; they have no reason to fear.

Prayer

Heavenly Father, when I see the evil around me, I am afraid. Forgive me for not trusting You completely. Keep my mind focused on Jesus so that I may praise and serve You without fear. I pray in the name of my Savior. Amen.

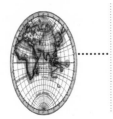

As they approached Jerusalem and came to Bethphage on the Mount of Olives, Jesus sent two disciples, saying to them, "Go to the village ahead of you, and at once you will find a donkey tied there, with her colt by her. Untie them and bring them to Me. If anyone says anything to you, tell him that the Lord needs them, and he will send them right away." *Matthew 21:1–3*

Into the Word

Of course you know the characters in the Palm Sunday story: Jesus riding on the donkey, the children shouting "Hosanna," the crowd spreading their coats on the road and waving palm branches, even the Pharisees protesting the noisy demonstration. But what about the other character?

Somewhere on the edge of the village of Bethphage lived a man who owned a lowly donkey and its colt. One Sunday morning two strangers (disciples of Jesus, but the man had no way of knowing that) untied the animals and started to leave. When the man tried to stop them, they explained that the Lord needed them.

What would you do? Refuse to let the animals go? Send for the local authorities who deal with donkey rustling? Demand a further explanation?

The man from Bethphage did none of these. He simply sent them right away because the Lord needed them. Needed them so God's prophecy through Zechariah could be fulfilled. Needed them for the journey that would end on Calvary's hill. Needed them to begin the week that would end the domination of sin over the people of God.

God had given that man a donkey and a colt—because Jesus would need them. What does God need that He has given you?

God has given each of us talents and abilities. Some are gifted in music or art. Others make friends easily and are comfortable talking to people about their faith. Some people have a wealth of worldly gifts and the heart to share with those in need. Still others can hold the hand and wipe the tears of the hurting. What does God need that He has given you?

God has given each of us salvation through His Son, Jesus. Through Baptism He has given us new life. Through the Holy Spirit He has given us faith and nourishes that faith. What does God need that He has given you?

The Lord needs your donkey. Just what has He given you?

Prayer Thought

Thank God for all He has given you, especially salvation through His Son. Then ask Him to show you what you have been given that He needs to build His kingdom.

On reaching Jerusalem, Jesus entered the temple area and began driving out those who were buying and selling there. He overturned the tables of the money changers and the benches of those selling doves, and would not allow anyone to carry merchandise through the temple courts. And as He taught them, He said, "Is it not written: 'My house will be called a house of prayer for all nations'? But you have made it 'a den of robbers.'" *Mark 11:15–17*

Something to Think About

Everyone knew what was going on at the corner of Fifth and Main Street. Expensive cars from out of town cruising the neighborhood, stopping occasionally to check with the kids on the corner. Strangers hanging around at all hours with nothing to do, waiting to talk to the high school kids on their way home from school. Money changing hands, beepers buzzing, and long calls from the corner phone booth.

Everyone knew about the drug dealers at Fifth and Main, and everyone was angry. But no one knew what to do.

Dan and his friends were angry. They went to the city council meeting and demanded to know why the police had done nothing about the dealers. They organized an anti-drug group at school in which students pledged to avoid the drug dealers and not use drugs themselves. They asked the school administration to provide a meeting space for a support group to help students who had been through drug rehabilitation and were trying to stay drug-free.

Evan was angry too. One night he loaded the pistol his father kept in the nightstand drawer for security and drove to the corner of Fifth and Main. Evan shot and killed one of the drug dealers, a boy his own age, and wounded two students from his school.

Into the Word

Anger. It can be channeled to accomplish good or evil. It depends upon where you direct it.

Jesus was angry when He saw the money changers and merchants turning the temple into a den of robbers. Jesus, the Lord of the temple, drove them out and restored the building to a place of prayer and worship.

Jesus was angry about our sin. He didn't destroy us or leave us to the death that is always sin's consequence. Instead He destroyed sin and death for us by dying on the cross.

Prayer

Jesus, thank You for dying to forgive my sins. Help me to direct my anger against sin and injustice for Your sake. Amen.

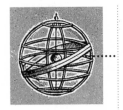

About an hour later another asserted, "Certainly this fellow was with Him, for he is a Galilean."

Peter replied, "Man, I don't know what you're talking about!" Just as he was speaking, the rooster crowed. The Lord turned and looked straight at Peter. Then Peter remembered the word the Lord had spoken to him: "Before the rooster crows today, you will disown Me three times." And he went outside and wept bitterly. *Luke 22:59–62*

Into the Word

Most people live in small- or middle-sized emotional boxes, alternating between "mostly happy" or "pretty good" and "kind of down" or "not so hot." But not Peter. His humongous box extended from mountaintops to the depths of despair.

Peter—who walked on the water of Galilee. Who confessed before the other disciples, "Lord, to whom shall we go? You have the words of eternal life" (John 6:68). Who wanted to build mountaintop shelters for Jesus, Moses, and Elijah. Who protested Jesus' service of foot washing in the Upper Room. Who fell asleep while Jesus agonized in prayer, and lashed out with drawn sword against the high priest's servant. Then, in the courtyard of the high priest's palace, he denied three times that he knew Jesus.

Peter, too confident in his own ability, could never have preached to thousands on Pentecost and led the infant Christian church. But at the rooster's crowing Peter discovered that without Jesus he was nothing at all. And he wept bitterly.

In My Life

Have you experienced highs and lows like Peter's? One minute full of confidence, ready to conquer the world on your own; the next shaken, overcome with feelings of inadequacy? School, athletics, dating, friendship—all these areas leave room for mercurial ascents and plunges.

We're happy to take the highs, feeling we somehow deserve them. But, oh, those lows! Can any good come from them?

It did for Peter. Shortly after His resurrection, Jesus met Peter on the beach. "Do you love Me?" He asked Peter three times. "Feed My lambs; feed My sheep." Peter knew what Jesus meant. He felt His loving forgiveness. He knew that Jesus would use him to build His church.

Through failure and bitter tears Peter had learned that Jesus—not Peter—had won salvation for all believers and that Jesus—not Peter—would build the church.

Prayer

Lord, I sometimes feel so confident that I could accomplish everything by myself. But in the next moment I realize how much I need You. Forgive my sins, and use me in Your kingdom for Jesus' sake. Amen.

When Jesus saw her weeping, and the Jews who had come along with her also weeping, He was deeply moved in spirit and troubled. "Where have you laid him?" He asked. "Come and see, Lord," they replied. Jesus wept. Then the Jews said, "See how He loved him." *John 11:33–36*

Something to Think About

Dear Advice Columnist,

You can't believe how embarrassed I feel. A bunch of us guys were hanging out in the gym after school. A kid I didn't know very well asked me about what happened to Craig. Craig was my best friend, you see, ever since kindergarten—closer to me than my own brother. I didn't want to talk about Craig, but he kept asking questions. So I started to explain how Craig and I were walking home from youth group, and this car going way too fast ran off the road on our side. It missed me, but hit Craig. Later that night at the hospital Craig died. The driver of the car was so drunk he could hardly stand up when the police arrested him.

The worst part is that, when I tried to tell the kid what happened, I started to cry and I couldn't stop. Now the other guys act like they're afraid to be seen with me. Who can I talk to who will understand?

Bruce

Dear Bruce,

It's really sad that boys grow up thinking that crying or showing other emotions is unmanly. Actually it takes a brave human being—male or female—to express and deal with emotions.

Jesus lost a good friend too. By the time He got to Bethany, Lazarus had been dead for four days. When Jesus saw Mary and Martha weeping, He was deeply moved. He shared their pain; He wept with them.

The amazing part is that Jesus knew what He was going to do, that in a few minutes He would bring Lazarus back to life. But death still brought pain; pain brought sadness; sadness brought tears.

You know that your friend, Craig, believed in Jesus and will live with Him forever. But his death still hurts. To deal with those emotions you will want to talk to Someone who has shared them, your Savior, Jesus Christ.

Prayer

Jesus, You have been a human being and felt the way I feel. Today I feel _____ . Help me to _____ . Thank You for understanding and caring about me, even caring enough to die for me. Amen.

A new command I give you: Love one another. As I have loved you, so you must love one another. By this all men will know that you are My disciples, if you love one another.
John 13:34-35

Something to Think About

"I love you, Mom," called Cindy as she slammed the back door on her way out. Mom sighed and looked around the kitchen. The sink overflowed with the dishes Cindy had promised to wash before she left. On the table lay Cindy's unopened school books.

"You know I love you, Brad," Dad said. Then he went on to explain how his important business trip next week would mean postponing their camping trip again. He didn't even ask about Brad's basketball game last Friday, the one he had promised he'd come home to watch.

"I love you, Stacey," whispered Pete as he pulled Stacey closer in the backseat of his car. Then he tried to show her exactly what he thought she should do if she loved him as much as he loved her. After all, Pete thought, what good is love if it doesn't get you something that feels good?

Into the Word

After supper on the night before He was going to die, Jesus told His disciples, "A new command I give you: Love one another."

"Easy," thought the disciples. "We're already doing that—at least, most of the time."

But Jesus wasn't finished. "As I have loved you, so you must love one another."

As He had loved them? That was a different matter. He was their Teacher and Lord who had patiently explained again and again about His kingdom. This very evening He, their Master, had humbly washed their feet. Then in the bread and wine of the new testament, He gave them His body and blood.

Within the next 24 hours He would be betrayed and taken prisoner without defending Himself, condemned on the testimony of false witnesses without saying a word in His own behalf, and nailed to a Roman cross to die. All this because of love so great that it caused Him to die in the place of His friends.

In My Life

What did "I love you" mean to Cindy, Dad, and Pete?

What do the words "I love you" mean to you? Measure your meaning of *love* against Jesus' example. You'll find another excellent description of love like His in 1 Corinthians 13.

Prayer

Lord Jesus, You loved me enough to die for my sins. Help me to love others as You have loved me. Amen.

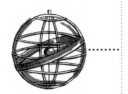

Fear the LORD, you His saints, for those who fear Him lack nothing. The lions may grow weak and hungry, but those who seek the LORD lack no good thing. *Psalm 34:9–10*

Something to Think About

Juanita hummed a tune from church as she heated the soup on the ancient hot plate. As soon as the soup was warm, she would spoon it into unmatched bowls for her little brothers.

As Juanita and the boys bowed their heads to thank God for the food, Mrs. Martinez from the next apartment opened the door. "Your Mama called," she told Juanita. "She asked me to come over and tell you she got some overtime, so she won't be home for a couple hours."

Juanita smiled as she thought about the extra money Mama would earn. Because she spoke only a little English and had no education, Mama had had a hard time finding work. The overtime pay would help them catch up on bills, and Juanita didn't mind staying home every night with her brothers.

After supper Juanita helped the boys finish their homework. Then she put them to bed in the tiny bedroom they shared with her and Mama. "People who have televisions and stereos must have a much harder time getting the children to go to bed," Juanita chuckled to herself. "Sleeping three in a bed sounds pretty inviting to little boys in this cold, quiet apartment."

Into the Word

We could easily make a long list of things that Juanita lacks. But Juanita doesn't see it that way. She would agree with the psalmist that "those who seek the LORD lack no good thing" (Psalm 34:10). She trusts God to take care of her and provide for her needs, just as He has always done in the past.

Juanita knows that our deepest need is for God and His forgiveness. He sent Jesus to take the punishment for our sins by dying on the cross. His Holy Spirit gives us faith to believe in Him and live for Him. We can bring our needs to Him in prayer, confident that He will answer us with all good things.

In My Life

Sometimes we fail to see how well God has provided for our needs because we confuse "needs" with "wants." The next time you feel God hasn't provided something you need, ask yourself

1. Is this really a need?
2. Is this really good for me?
3. Is this the best time for me to have this? Why might God want me to wait?

Prayer Thought

Thank God for providing for all your needs, especially your need for a Savior from sin. Ask Him to help you to be content with what you have.

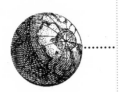

He chose David His servant and took him from the sheep pens; from tending the sheep He brought him to be the shepherd of His people Jacob, of Israel His inheritance. And David shepherded them with integrity of heart; with skillful hands he led them. *Psalm 78:70–72*

Into the Word

Being a shepherd may have been a lot of things, but it certainly wasn't high-profile or glamorous.

David knew. As the youngest son of Jesse, David spent his childhood years in the fields near Bethlehem, tending his father's sheep. His older brothers went off to be warriors, but not young David. Someone had to be with the sheep.

So, day after day and year after year, David moved the herd from one place to another to provide green pastures and quiet waters. He fought off and killed lions and bears with only his bare hands to save the lives of the sheep entrusted to his care. Confident of their shepherd's care, Jesse's sheep grazed well and prospered. (In Psalm 23 David gives us a picture of the shepherd's work.)

Shepherding doesn't sound like administrative training for future kings, but that was exactly God's plan for David. Anointed by Samuel, David became king of God's people Israel. As he had once fought lions and bears, with God's help he bravely faced the armies of King Saul and of Israel's enemies. As he had provided for the needs of the sheep, so he governed the people entrusted to his care. Through King David God blessed His people, Israel, and they prospered.

David, the shepherd king, was the picture God gave His people of the royal Shepherd from the house of David who would one day come to rule. "I am the good Shepherd. The good Shepherd lays down His life for the sheep," Jesus said (John 10:11). He has saved us from our worst enemies, sin and death, and under His care we prosper.

In My Life

What are you doing today that seems menial? Baby-sitting? Schoolwork? Household chores? Helping a younger brother or sister with homework? Pet-sitting for a neighbor?

This week make a list of all the unglamorous, low-profile chores or activities you do. Then ask yourself: How could God be using this to prepare me for what He has planned for me to do?

Prayer

Forgive me, Lord, for grumbling about the things I have to do. Help me to see Your plan in my life and in all that happens to me. Help me to trust You to use everything for my good. In the name of Jesus my Savior. Amen.

At first His disciples did not understand all this. Only after Jesus was glorified did they realize that these things had been written about Him and that they had done these things to Him. *John 12:16*

In My Life

It's always perfectly clear in hindsight, although you certainly didn't understand why it happened at the time. You decide on the basis of a funny dream you've had to register for Spanish class instead of French, and the teacher seats you alphabetically in front of a girl you've never met. Or, you go along with a friend and his youth group to help with a party at a homeless shelter. Seemingly insignificant incidents at the time. But looking back many years later, when you marry the girl from Spanish class or graduate with a degree in social work, you see God's plan and purpose actively carried out in your life.

Into the Word

Jesus' disciples spent three years accompanying Him as He healed the sick and preached the good news about the kingdom of God to the people of Israel. They tasted the wine He had miraculously made from water, shared in the bread and fish with which He fed 5,000 people, stared in amazement as He cast out evil spirits and brought the dead back to life. They marched in the Palm Sunday procession into Jerusalem and fled in terror from Gethsemane. But it was not until after the resurrection that they realized that Jesus had fulfilled exactly what the Old Testament prophets had said He would do.

Can you imagine Peter chained in a cell in Rome? Or John, an old man on the island of Patmos? How often they must have looked back to the days they had spent with Jesus, listening to His words and watching His miracles. How clearly the details fit, now that they knew the risen Christ. Through the coming of the Holy Spirit on Pentecost, the disciples understood God's plan and purpose—the salvation of all people through Jesus' death and resurrection. And once they understood, they shared the Good News with everyone.

Something to Think About

As you grow older, you will have many opportunities to look back and see how God worked out His plan and purpose in your life.

Talk to an older Christian—one of your grandparents, a neighbor, or a friend from your church. Ask them to tell you what they now see, looking back, that God has done for them that they didn't understand at the time it happened.

Prayer

I don't know, Lord, what the future holds for me, but I do know that You hold my future. Because You have made me Your child through Jesus, I know my future is in good hands. Amen.

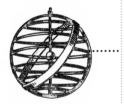

Paul and his companions traveled throughout the region of Phrygia and Galatia, having been kept by the Holy Spirit from preaching the word in the province of Asia. *Acts 16:6*

Into the Word

Don't you wonder how Paul knew? Luke, the writer of Acts, tells us the Holy Spirit prevented Paul from preaching in Asia at this time, but he doesn't explain how it happened. Was it a vision? The advice of a trusted friend? Or a road construction project that blocked his travel? However the message came, Paul understood and went on to Troas where God called him to come over to Macedonia, and Paul's ministry on the continent of Europe was launched.

In My Life

If you're like most of us, you don't hear voices from heaven or get directions in visions. So how will you know if something is or isn't God's will? Four Christian friends offer some advice.

"Last year some of my friends had begun to use marijuana. They invited me to try it too. They even joked that marijuana was one of the plants God had made so He must want us to enjoy it. I was confused. But I remembered reading in His word that my body is a temple of the Holy Spirit (1 Corinthians

6:19). If God cared so much about me that He sent His Son to save me, it must be His will that I take care of my body and not use harmful drugs." —Jeff

"I was having a hard time deciding what career to prepare for. I didn't know if God wanted me to be an engineer or a math teacher or something else. So I had a long talk with Mr. Phillips from my church. He helped me see that God had given me a real love for children that would make me an excellent teacher. He asked me to help with his Sunday school class to get some experience." —Susan

"I've always loved music, and I started playing the organ in church occasionally when I was still in junior high. I believe it's God's will for my life that I serve Him professionally as a church musician. I know I'd make much more money doing something else. But then my career choice would be motivated by greed, and choices made with that kind of motivation are never God's will." —Adrian

"My church is starting a new teen center where young people can come after school or in the evening for Christian fun, fellowship, Bible study, and service projects. I pledged to contribute financially to building the center. The next week the owner of a gas station called to offer me a job. I know my pledge was in keeping with God's will because He provided the funds for me to do it." —Peter

Prayer

Dear Lord, You have redeemed me through Jesus' death so I could live for You. Help me to see Your will for me and live according to it. Amen.

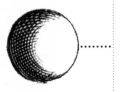

While Jesus was having dinner at Levi's [Matthew's] house, many tax collectors and "sinners" were eating with Him and His disciples, for there were many who followed Him.
Mark 2:15

Into the Word

That's it—the example you've been look-ing for! Jesus at a party with "many tax collectors and sinners"! So partying is good, and my parents won't be able to object anymore, right?

Something to Think About

If partying is good, why does it have such a bad reputation? Should Christian young people go to parties or not? Before deciding, ask yourself a few questions.

Why do I want to go? If getting drunk or experimenting with drugs or sex is your motive for going to a party, then God wouldn't want you to go. He loves you—body and soul—enough to send His only Son, Jesus, to suffer and die for you, and your body is precious to Him.

Do you want to party so that you will be accepted by the "popular" people? Acting in a way that is harmful to you physically or spiritually is too high a price to pay for acceptance. And you already have the acceptance of God, Himself, who accepts you because of what Jesus has done for you.

Do you want to get to know more people and have fun with them? That can be a good motive for going, if you're not afraid to let them see the real you, the one that belongs to Jesus. If you're intimidated into behaving in a sinful manner, no one will see your light shining. Getting to know you should mean eventually getting to know your Savior, Jesus. You don't have to preach a sermon at the first meeting, but you should leave an impression that somehow shows you have experienced the love of Christ.

Is the party you want to attend likely to present a temptation you can't handle? Harmful behaviors—smoking, drinking, drugs, sex—seem far less harmful in a party atmosphere. Know your own breaking point, and don't test it. You may want to go with a Christian friend so you can encourage each other.

Will your reputation be damaged by attending the party? People who know you are a Christian are watching you to see what you do. Even if you do nothing wrong, they may presume you're guilty just because you were there.

What would your parents think about the party? If you would have to lie to them in order to go, you don't belong there.

Prayer

Lord Jesus, You were young too and enjoyed being with Your friends. Help me to remember I am Your redeemed child in all that I say and do so that I may bring glory to You, my Savior. Amen.

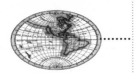

For You created my inmost being;
You knit me together in my mother's
womb. I praise You because I am
fearfully and wonderfully made; Your
works are wonderful, I know that
full well. *Psalm 139:13–14*

Something to Think About

Everyone at school knew Lori's reputation. Most of the girls avoided her, afraid that other people might think they did the same kind of things she did. The boys talked about her a lot, and sometimes two or three would gather around her locker to joke or make plans. But most of the guys she saw in the evening felt embarrassed to be seen talking with her at school.

Even the teachers didn't pay much attention to Lori. They all knew she had had a baby at the end of school last year, and rumors said she was pregnant again. It seemed pointless to waste a lot of time on Lori when she'd never amount to anything anyway.

Lori closed her locker and left school alone, as usual. When she reached the student parking lot, she heard a car horn. She looked up to see Chad smiling at her from his car. "Why not," shrugged Lori, "I'm not good for anything else. At least somebody will like me for a little while." And she got in the car with Chad. Or was it Rich?

Into the Word

"I'm okay—God doesn't make junk." That was the message on the bright yellow button the child wore to preschool. And that's what God, speaking through the psalmist in Psalm 139, says about us.

He made us in His own image, felt as proud of us as the father whose child "looks just like his old man." But our first parents chose to disobey God, and through their sin lost His image. Although God hated our sin, He loved us so much that He sent His own Son to become a human being, live on earth, and die for sin in our place. God not only made us, He has redeemed us to be His own.

In My Life

If God, our Creator and Redeemer, has that much respect for us, shouldn't we show respect for our own bodies? Because we are His, we eat nutritious food and get the rest our bodies require. We keep ourselves clean and follow the doctor's directions when we are ill. We will not hurt the body God has made and redeemed by using harmful substances such as alcohol, tobacco,. or drugs. And we look forward to enjoying God's gift of sex in marriage as He planned.

Prayer

Dear Lord, forgive me for sinning against my own body. Help me to respect my body as You did when You died to redeem me. Amen.

Two men went up to the temple to pray, one a Pharisee and the other a tax collector. The Pharisee stood up and prayed about himself: "God, I thank You that I am not like other men—robbers, evildoers, adulterers— or even like this tax collector. I fast twice a week and give a tenth of all I get."

But the tax collector stood at a distance. He would not even look up to heaven, but beat his breast and said, "God, have mercy on me, a sinner." *Luke 18:10–13*

Something to Think About

The sports reporter for the school newspaper interviewed Megan and Kristi for an article he was writing. "Both of you have had outstanding seasons," he said, "and you're both in line to be named 'Swimmer of the Year.' To what do you owe your success?"

Megan answered first. "I've always been really good at sports. It seems like I just know what to do. I practice really hard, and it pays off for me. Sure, my times have been a little slower the past few weeks, but I'm going to be sensational at the state meet."

Then came Kristi's turn. "I'm thankful for the strong, healthy body God has given me. My swimming has improved so much this season under Coach Parks' instruction. I try to incorporate all his suggestions when I practice my starts and turns. I'm really grateful for all he's done for me, and I'll try my hardest to repay him by swimming well at the state meet."

Later the reporter covered the Athletic Awards Night when Coach Parks presented the

"Swimmer of the Year" award. "Coachability has been the key to the success of this year's winner," he said. "She was a fairly good swimmer at the beginning of the season. But instead of relying only on her natural ability, she listened to everyone who tried to help her and learned from both her coaches and teammates. When her competition began to have problems, she continued to improve. I'm proud to announce that Kristi is our 'Swimmer of the Year.' "

Into the Word

Like Megan, the Pharisee in Jesus' parable believed he alone was responsible for all he was—a good and righteous man in the eyes of others. But God saw what he really was, a sinner who could not save himself. The tax collector acknowledged his sinfulness and relied on God for forgiveness. Jesus said, "... this man, rather than the other, went home justified before God. For everyone who exalts himself will be humbled, and he who humbles himself will be exalted" (Luke 18:14).

In My Life

In what area of your life have you been taking all the credit? How can you give God the glory?

Prayer

God, have mercy on me, a sinner. Forgive me and count me righteous for the sake of Your Son, Jesus. Amen.

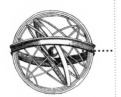

When Jesus saw him lying there and learned that he had been in this condition for a long time, He asked him, "Do you want to get well?"
John 5:6

Something to Think About

The convicted child molester had served his time with good behavior and the prison system of Texas was about to release him on parole. But the prisoner protested, promising that he would begin to molest children again as soon as he had the opportunity. Was the prisoner afraid to leave the world behind bars to which he had become accustomed? Or, was he afraid he would be unable to stop the destructive pattern of behavior for which he had been imprisoned?

Into the Word

"Do you want to get well?" The disabled man had laid beside the Pool of Bethesda for 38 years. What kind of a question was that for Jesus to ask?

But the man's excuses make us wonder. "I have no one to help me into the pool when the water is stirred. While I am trying to get in, someone else goes down ahead of me." In other words, "Lord, it's someone else's fault, so for 38 years I've laid here and made excuses. It's not a great life, but at least it's one with which I'm very familiar."

"Get up," said Jesus. "Pick up your mat and walk." Excuses and other people had not been able to break the man free from his disability. But touched by the grace of God he was healed.

In My Life

What is disabling or imprisoning you? Is it an attitude of defeatism or perfectionism? Is it self-love that puts your desires above everything and everyone else? Is it a "pet" sin that you enjoy so much or that has become so much a part of you that you can't give it up?

Maybe you've tried to change. Your own efforts might have worked for a while, but then you found yourself reverting to your old ways. It's not a great life, but it is one with which you're very familiar.

But God has touched you with His grace, forgiven you for the sake of His Son, Jesus Christ, who suffered and died to free you from your sins. Through the Holy Spirit He gives you the power to "pick up your mat and walk"—to leave behind the old ways that disabled and imprisoned you and to walk in newness of life.

Prayer

Amazing grace! How sweet the sound
That saved a wretch like me!
I once was lost but now am found,
Was blind but now I see! Amen.

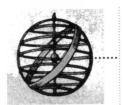

As He went along, He saw a man blind from birth. His disciples asked Him, "Rabbi, who sinned, this man or his parents, that he was born blind?"

"Neither this man nor his parents sinned," said Jesus, "but this happened so that the work of God might be displayed in his life." *John 9:1–3*

Into the Word

To our scientifically trained minds, these verses sound primitive. The disciples see a blind man begging along the side of the road and immediately assume his blindness is the result of sin. "Who sinned, this man or his parents, that he was born blind?"

The disciples' question reflected the principle of the rabbis that "there is no death without sin, and there is no suffering without iniquity." The rabbis also taught that terrible punishments came on certain people because of their parents' sin.

Jesus made it plain that He did not agree. "Neither this man nor his parents sinned, but this happened so that the work of God might be displayed in his life." Then Jesus spit on the ground, made a little mud with the saliva, and put it on the man's eyes, instructing him to wash at the Pool of Siloam. When the man returned from the pool, he could see.

Neighbors noticed, asked questions, and spread the wonderful news. The Pharisees heard and called for an investigation. The man and his parents testified. As he explained what had happened, the man who now could see realized that the Rabbi who had given him sight was the Son of God.

In My Life

How often we have echoed the disciples' "primitive" question! When bad things happen to us, our first thought is "What did I do to deserve this?" (Since we take credit for all the good things that happen to us, it's a logical assumption, isn't it?)

But this mentality puts the focus on the sufferer and his suffering instead of on the Savior. Jesus restored the blind man's sight—exactly what the Old Testament prophets had said the Messiah would do. Because God's power was demonstrated in this miracle, many people were forced to consider whether the Healer, Jesus, could be the one God had promised to send.

When you face suffering in your life or in the lives of people you love, look to the Savior instead of the suffering, and to the glory that God will reveal through this suffering. As Paul wrote to the Roman Christians suffering persecution for their faith, "I consider that our present sufferings are not worth comparing with the glory that will be revealed in us" (Romans 8:18).

Prayer

Lord, help me to see that You will be glorified through my suffering. Give me the patience to endure and to witness to Your goodness, especially in saving me from my sins. Amen.

My eyes will be on the faithful in the land, that they may dwell with me; he whose walk is blameless will minister to me. *Psalm 101:6*

Something to Think About

Who are your heroes—the people you most admire? Are they professional athletes? movie or TV stars? popular recording artists? political leaders?

Many people look up to professional athletes because of their physical skills. Their fans may also be attracted by their huge salaries and the lifestyles those salaries finance.

Fame attracts many people to movie, TV, and recording stars. The media is quick to focus on their glamorous lives, full of parties and associations with other famous people. Their work appears to provide an endless supply of money to be used for their pleasure.

Besides fame, political heroes seem to possess a great deal of power. The future of the world is affected by their every decision. Most of us would like to wield that kind of power.

Your hero is someone you would like to be like. For that reason it's important to know what your hero's beliefs and values are.

Into the Word

David, the writer of Psalm 101, had been anointed king of Israel. Yet he was looking for heroes—people he could look to as examples as he ruled.

David set criteria for these heroes. They must be faithful—faithful to God, that is, exhibiting high moral integrity. Their walk must be blameless: They must live by God's law in all they do. David goes on to say that in his administration he will not tolerate men who make their way by double-dealing. He promises to destroy all the wicked—those who slander their neighbors and are motivated by pride—in the Lord's kingdom.

In My Life

What criteria have you set for choosing your heroes? Think of someone you admire and would like to be like. Then ask yourself the following questions about that person:

- What do I admire about this person?
- What qualities has this person shown that I would like to imitate?
- What has this person's life shown about his beliefs and values?
- In what way has this person shown that he does or doesn't believe in Jesus?

Then ask yourself the same questions about that ultimate Hero, Jesus Christ.

Prayer Thought

Ask God to lead you to choose heroes who will help you in your walk with Him.

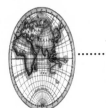

Praise be to You, O Lord; teach me Your decrees. With my lips I recount all the laws that come from Your mouth. I rejoice in following Your statutes as one rejoices in great riches. *Psalm 119:12–14*

Something to Think About

Rules! I hate rules! Life would be so much better without them. Wouldn't it?

Or would it? Stop and think, for example, what driving a car would be like without the Rules of the Road. Accidents would clog every intersection because no one would know who had the right-of-way. Speeding cars in congested areas would be a threat to pedestrians. Drivers would constantly have to watch for on-coming traffic in their lane.

Rules (or laws) help our society function in an orderly manner for the good of all. Banking rules ensure that our money will still be on deposit when we need to withdraw it from our savings account. Child labor laws protect children from being exploited for profit.

Into the Word

The writer of Psalm 119 praises God for His Law. He says he rejoices in following the rules God has given the same way he would rejoice in great riches.

God's Law serves as a guide for our lives. It tells us that we should love God above everything else. It teaches us to love our neighbors as we love ourselves. When we follow God's Law, we live in harmony with Him and with our neighbors.

The Law acts as a curb to sin. By keeping check on excessive violence and wickedness in society, the Law makes possible an atmosphere of order and safety.

The Law also serves as a mirror. When we study God's Law, we see clearly how badly we have failed to keep it. And we realize that no matter how hard we try, we will never meet the Law's standards.

Only one Person has ever kept the Law perfectly. Jesus Christ, God's Son, became a human being and kept the Law, just as God demanded. Not for His own sake, of course, because He was God. But Jesus kept God's Law in our place. Then He was crucified to pay the price of all of our sins against the Law. He gives us His righteousness as a free gift, which we receive by faith.

73

Prayer

God, I thank You for Your Law. I know that I have not kept it and am incapable of keeping it on my own. Thank You for sending Jesus to obey the Law for me and to die in my place. Amen.

Are not two sparrows sold for a penny? Yet not one of them will fall to the ground apart from the will of your Father. And even the very hairs of your head are all numbered. So don't be afraid; you are worth more than many sparrows. *Matthew 10:29–31*

Something to Think About

What are you worth? A scientist once calculated the value of each of the elements found in the body of an average-sized adult. The total—a little less than a dollar.

Into the Word

Jesus compared the value of a human being to the price of sparrows: "Are not two sparrows sold for a penny? Yet not one of them will fall to the ground apart from the will of Your Father. ... You are worth more than many sparrows" (Matthew 10:29–31):

God backs up His evaluation of your worth with His constant attention, from the moment of your conception until He receives you in heaven at your death. He provides for your every need: food, clothing, shelter, family, friends, a healthy body, and mind with which you can learn and earn a living. Jesus said, "Even the very hairs of your head are all numbered" (Matthew 10:30).

God proved beyond all doubt how much He cares for you. He sent His only Son into the world to suffer and die for your sins, to take your punishment so you will not die, but will live with Him forever. To understand what you are worth to God, read the words of John 3:16 aloud, putting your name in the blank spaces: "For God so loved [_____] that He gave His one and only Son, that [_____ who] believes in Him shall not perish but have eternal life."

In My Life

Since you are worth so much to God, He'll surely take away all your troubles, right? Wrong!

Jesus says you will have even more troubles because you belong to Him. "I am sending you out like sheep among wolves," He told His disciples (Matthew 10:16). "If the world hates you, keep in mind that it hated Me first" (John 15:18). But He promises His blessing when we suffer for His sake: "Blessed are you when people insult you, persecute you and falsely say all kinds of evil against you because of Me. Rejoice and be glad, because great is your reward in heaven" (Matthew 5:11–12).

The real test of something's value is how well it holds up under pressure and over time. "Be faithful, even to the point of death, and I will give you the crown of life" (Revelation 2:10).

Prayer

Heavenly Father, I don't deserve the value You have placed on me. Help me to remember that You have made me precious in Your sight through the blood of Your Son. Amen.

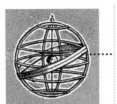

When the Son of Man comes in His glory, and all the angels with Him, He will sit on His throne in heavenly glory. The King will reply, "I tell you the truth, whatever you did for one of the least of these brothers of Mine, you did for Me."
Matthew 25:31, 40

Something to Think About

Conrad the Cobbler could think of nothing else. In his dream Jesus had told him He would come to his shop today. Conrad had cleaned and cooked a fine meal. "I love Jesus so much, and I can't wait to do something nice for Him," thought Conrad.

At midmorning the door to the shop opened. Conrad rushed to greet Jesus. But only a poor girl with no shoes stood there. Conrad picked out his finest pair in her size and helped her put them on her feet.

Just before lunch the door opened again, and Conrad ran to greet his guest. But it was only a homeless woman, tired and thin from hunger. Conrad led her to his table where he served her the fine meal he had cooked for Jesus.

By late afternoon Conrad had almost given up. The door to the shop opened a third time and a crying boy entered. "I'm lost, and I can't find my way home," he sobbed. So Conrad locked up the shop and took the boy home to his mother.

That night a disappointed Conrad knelt by

his bed and prayed. "Lord, why didn't You come to my shop today? I wanted to do something nice for You."

Then Conrad heard the Lord answer, "But, Conrad, I did come. And you did three very nice things for Me. When I was barefoot, you gave Me a new pair of shoes. When I was hungry, you gave Me something to eat. And when I was lost, you helped Me find My way home."

In My Life

On that glorious day when Christ returns to earth to judge all people, you and I will stand before Him. He will separate the sheep from the goats, the saved from the damned.

You don't have to wonder where you will be. You believe that God has saved you by His grace through the suffering and death of Jesus. His judgment: By grace you are saved.

But the evidence? "Whatever you did for one of the least of these brothers of Mine, you did for Me" (Matthew 25:40).

Prayer

Forgive my sins, Lord, for Jesus' sake, that I may be judged righteous when You come again. Amen.

Now Peter was sitting out in the courtyard, and a servant girl came to him. "You also were with Jesus of Galilee," she said.

But he denied it before them all. "I don't know what you're talking about," he said. He denied it again, with an oath: "I don't know the Man!" Then he began to call down curses on himself and he swore to them, "I don't know the Man!"

Matthew 26:69–70, 72, 74

Into the Word

Poor, pressured Peter. He wanted to do the right thing to help his Master. In the garden, when the temple guard appeared, he had lashed out with his sword, wounding the high priest's servant. But Jesus hadn't appreciated his effort—in fact, He had reattached the servant's ear. Then Peter followed the guards and their Prisoner to the high priest's house. He would watch and wait, in case an opportunity arose. At least he would be able to see what happened. He joined the servants warming themselves around a fire in the courtyard. And then Peter panicked.

Peter's denial came in three stages. First he pretended he didn't know what they were talking about, tried to blend into the group and be just like them. His second denial was clear and to the point: "I don't know the Man!" But the third denial carried all the guilty fury of a man who has just lashed out against his best Friend. Calling down curses upon himself for what he had done, Peter swore again that he didn't even know Jesus.

In My Life

Remembering the three stages of Peter's denial may help you to realize what you are doing when you begin to deny Jesus. Do you recognize yourself in the following situations?

- Molly's friends are going skiing Sunday morning. They haven't invited her because they know her family goes to church. "I don't go every week," Molly tells them, "just when there's nothing else to do. Skiing's no problem."

- Jeff's friends are swearing and using foul language. Their conversation stops when Jeff comes in. "What the *!#%& is going on?" asks Jeff. "It's so ^*#@**! quiet in here!"

- Jenny hopped out of Dad's car and walked toward the theater where her friends waited. When no one could see her, she pulled off her cross necklace and put it in her pocket.

- Peter cried bitter tears of repentance, and Jesus forgave him and sent him out to witness for Him. His forgiveness waits for us when we repent after denying Him too.

Prayer

Jesus, forgive me when I, like Peter, pretend I don't know You. Give me the faith and the power to be a witness for You. Amen.

Jesus said, "A man was going down from Jerusalem to Jericho, when he fell into the hands of robbers ... "
Luke 10:30ff

Into the Word

Matthias, a reporter for the Jerusalem Herald, recently interviewed several people who were involved in an incident on the Jericho road. Let's read the notes from his interviews:

Alleged thieves: It appears someone ambushed this salesman on his way to Jericho and took all his money. Maybe it was us; maybe it wasn't—we're innocent until proven guilty. Anyway it's no affair of ours. People should know better than to go alone into areas like that.

Priest and Levite: Yes, we did travel the Jericho road yesterday, but we always keep our eyes straight ahead and probably didn't see anyone. I'm sure we didn't see him. Besides, he was such a bloody mess, we would have soiled our robes and been late to church if we had stopped.

Samaritan: I got off my donkey as soon as I heard his cries. The poor guy—the thieves had taken everything he had and beaten him up pretty bad. I'm sure they thought he was dead. I felt so sorry for him that I wanted to do whatever I could to help.

Innkeeper: In the field of hospitality and tourism, you're always happy to see a paying customer. But in this case the customer didn't pay his own bill—the Samaritan who brought him in paid it. You know, I don't understand that guy. He stayed up all night caring for the Jewish fellow, and you know how those Jews hate Samaritans.

Lawyer: When I asked Jesus about inheriting eternal life, it was a hypothetical question, the kind we lawyers are so fond of asking. But the story He told made me stop and think. The way that Samaritan helped the injured man—why, he loved him so much it's hard for me to understand. That must be what the law means when it says, "Love your neighbor as yourself."

Jesus: Go and do likewise.

In My Life

To love someone else as much as you love yourself is not humanly possible. Jesus, alone, accomplished this. He left His throne in heaven, was made Man, took our sins upon Himself, and died on the cross. Freed from sin's control by Jesus' blood, He gives us the power to really love one another.

Prayer

Forgive my sins, Lord Jesus, and give me the power to love others as You have loved me. Amen.

[Jesus said,] "But the hand of him who is going to betray Me is with Mine on the table." They began to question among themselves which of them it might be who would do this. Also a dispute arose among them as to which of them was considered to be greatest. *Luke 22:21,23-24*

Into the Word

The drama that began in the Garden of Eden nears its climax. Jesus sits at the Passover table with His disciples. He has just instituted a new testament with them, offering them with bread and wine His own body and blood for the forgiveness of their sins. Then comes the shocking news that one of them—His innermost circle of friends and followers—would soon betray Him to His enemies, and as it was decreed by God.

They're only a few hours away from the trials and scourging, the painful march to Calvary, and His awful crucifixion. All of time and eternity turns on this night and that day.

And what are the disciples talking about? The same old "I'm the greatest"—"No, I am better than you" they've been arguing about for the past three years!

In My Life

"Ridiculous," you say. "If I had been there, I'd have asked Jesus to tell me exactly what was going to happen. I would ask Him to give me the strength to stay with Him through His suffering. I would praise and adore Him for what He was about to do ..."

But would you? Or, would you have been right in there trading insults with the disciples? After all, they were simply focusing on their own concerns instead of on Jesus.

Make a list on paper of the 10 things you are most concerned about today. Is God's work or His kingdom even on your list?

Now use your imagination to put yourself 20 years into the future. Read your list again. Are these concerns still important, or do they seem petty and inappropriate when viewed from a distance of 20 years away?

The disciples ran in terror from the garden. Peter denied Jesus and only John witnessed the crucifixion. Yet Jesus loved and forgave these selfish cowards, gave them the gift of the Holy Spirit, and used them to build His church. Just as He does you and me.

Prayer

Lord, forgive me for focusing on my own concerns instead of on You. Change me, Lord, and use me in Your kingdom. Amen.

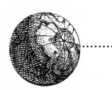

And beginning with Moses and all the Prophets, He explained to them what was said in all the Scriptures concerning Himself. Then He opened their minds so they could understand the Scriptures. *Luke 24:27, 45*

Into the Word

It wasn't easy to be a disciple those first few weeks after Easter.

Put yourself in the place of the two men walking home to Emmaus the evening of Easter Day. On the one hand, years of synagogue education had taught them all the words of the prophets concerning the coming Messiah. On the other hand, they had experienced the events in Jerusalem the past 72 hours: Jesus' betrayal and trials, His crucifixion and death, and now the wild rumors of His resurrection. But they never connected what they knew.

In frustration the disciples revealed their confusion to Jesus, the "stranger" who had joined their conversation. "How foolish you are," He chided them, "and how slow of heart to believe all that the prophets have spoken! Did not the Christ have to suffer these things and then enter His glory?" (Luke 24:25–26). And Jesus explained to them how the events in Jerusalem had fulfilled the words of the prophets.

Days later He did the same for the rest of

the disciples, opening their minds so they could understand the Scriptures.

In My Life

You want to read and study the Bible which you know to be the Word of God. But the Bible is long, written too long ago to understand today, seemingly disconnected, irrelevant, confusing (check one or more, or add your own).

Do what those disciples did. Turn your confusion over to the Expert. He has promised to give you the Holy Spirit to help you understand what you read and study and to help you grow in faith.

Make use of the "helps" in your Bible: study notes for books of the Bible or for individual verses, references to related texts, the concordance to find other passages using the same word, Bible dictionary, subject index, and atlas. If your Bible doesn't include these, you might consider buying one that does, as well as a basic Bible commentary.

The Holy Spirit often works through other believers. Don't hesitate to ask them for help when you are confused. It's worth the effort to understand—the Bible brings us the good news that Jesus, the Son of God, died to save us from our sins.

Prayer

Lord, I want to learn more about You and what You did for me. Open my mind so that I better understand Your Word. Amen.

The royal official said, "Sir, come down before my child dies." Jesus replied, "You may go. Your son will live." The man took Jesus at His word and departed. *John 4:49–50*

Something to Think About

Spring and summer had been hot and dry with almost no rain falling during the months of May and June. The farmers knew that if rain came now, their crops could revive; if the drought continued, the year's income would be lost.

So the members of the little country congregation met in a special prayer service to seek God's help. Petitions for rain were interspersed with hymns of faith in God's power to answer prayer: "Come, my soul, with every care, Jesus loves to answer prayer; He Himself bids you to pray, Therefore will not turn away."

As they finished singing the hymn, lightning pierced the leaden sky and torrents of rain soaked the worshipers exiting the church. Not one had brought an umbrella.

Into the Word

The royal official whose son was ill believed. "[He] took Jesus at His word and departed" (John 4:50), confident that a healthy child would greet him when he returned home. This was no Sunday morning faith limited to the interior of one's own church between the hours of 10:00 and 11:00 A.M. This faith hit the road, trusting enough to obey, never considering the "what ifs" or "impossibles."

In My Life

What about you? Do you take Jesus at His Word?

He promised to hear and answer your prayers, knowing your needs before you even ask and providing for them. Do you worry about the future, or do you go to God in prayer, confident that your life is safely in His almighty hands?

He promised to be with you always, to empower you with His Holy Spirit as you witness for Him. Do you continue to worry about what others will think and say, or do you boldly live your faith, giving glory to God?

He died on the cross to take away your sins. Do you wallow in guilt, unable to forgive yourself, or do you take Him at His word that you are forgiven, free to forgive yourself and others?

He says He's coming again. Do you live only for today or look forward in joy to going home with Him forever?

Prayer

[Lord,] I do believe; help me overcome my unbelief! (Mark 9:24) Amen.

From this time many of His disciples turned back and no longer followed Him.

"You do not want to leave too, do you?" Jesus asked the Twelve.

Simon Peter answered Him, "Lord, to whom shall we go? You have the words of eternal life. We believe and know that You are the Holy One of God." *John 6:66–69*

Something to Think About

The combo had only a few minutes to set up their equipment before the contemporary worship service began. The crowd of worshipers streaming into the pews added to the tension and confusion.

The keyboard player plugged the speaker jacks into the keyboard and sat down to check the instrument by playing a few chords. Silence. She checked the switches on the keyboard and speakers to be sure they were all in the "on" position and tried another chord. Silence again. In panic she disconnected the speaker jacks and reversed them, then made sure all the electrical plugs were firmly inserted into the power strip outlet. Still silence. The keyboard would not play.

Finally a front-row worshiper who had been watching the whole procedure got up out of his seat and walked up to the keyboard. He picked up the end of the extension cord and plugged it into the wall outlet. The keyboard played, and the worship service could begin.

Into the Word

Peter had found the source of eternal life—Jesus Christ Himself, who would die on the cross to provide life for all who believe in Him. Peter spoke for all of the disciples, "Lord, to whom shall we go? You have the words of eternal life" (John 6:68).

In My Life

Peter speaks for us also. Through faith we too have come to know Jesus as the source of eternal life. Without Him we are disconnected from God, doomed to eternal separation from Him.

Like the disciples who had turned back and stopped following Jesus, many in our day look for other ways to find God. Some look for power in the cosmic forces or the harmony of nature. Others trust human intellect to work out a relationship with God on human terms. Still others seek salvation in world religions such as Buddhism or Hinduism.

Jesus made the source of eternal life very clear: "I am the Way and the Truth and the Life. No one comes to the Father except through Me" (John 14:6).

Prayer

Lord Jesus, thank You for revealing Yourself to me as the Source of eternal life. Keep me in this faith until I live with You forever in heaven. Amen.

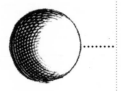

And we know that in all things God works for the good of those who love Him, who have been called according to His purpose. *Romans 8:28*

Something to Think About

"I just don't get it," grumbled Mr. Parker. "The preacher said everything was going to work out well, but look at the mess we're in. Just when we're starting to catch up on our debts, I lose my job. Now we'll never be able to buy that new boat I've been wanting. My wife's run off, my daughter's pregnant, and my son's in jail. If you call this good, I hope I never see bad!"

Into the Word

Poor Mr. Parker. Unfortunately he only remembered part of the Bible verse his pastor had read.

God works in all things, not just isolated incidents, for the good of those who love Him. Evil seems much more prevalent in our world than good. Unemployment, family problems, illness, and natural disasters happen to Christians too. But all of it works for our long-range good— remaining with God as His redeemed children.

In My Life

God isn't promising to make us happy, but rather to fulfill His purpose—to save sinners through Jesus. To fulfill that purpose the Holy Spirit works faith in your heart and empowers you to share the Good News of salvation with others. The Holy Spirit enables you to love and serve others the way Christ loves you.

You are special; this promise isn't for everyone. God has called you for His purpose through His Word and through the sacraments. He chose you before the foundation of the world to be made holy through the blood of His Son.

Through Word and Sacrament you have become a new person, with a new way of looking at things. Instead of worrying about the future, you trust in God to take care of you. Instead of striving to accumulate treasure on earth, you know that your security is in heaven, where earthly disasters cannot destroy your treasure.

When this new you, who is called according to God's purpose, experiences trouble and pain, you accept it instead of resenting it. You know that suffering is part of God's plan too and brings you closer to Him. So close that in the end you will spend eternity with Him in heaven.

Prayer

It's easy to trust You, Lord, when everything is going well. Help me to praise You even in suffering knowing that in all things You work for my good according to Your purpose. Amen.

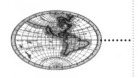

Do not conform any longer to the pattern of this world, but be transformed by the renewing of your mind. Then you will be able to test and approve what God's will is—His good, pleasing and perfect will. *Romans 12:2*

Something to Think About

Has it ever happened at your school? One lone person decides he's tired of conforming to the current trend and dares to be different. Maybe he wears loafers to school instead of high tops; perhaps he shows up in a neat shirt and tie instead of the standard T-shirt. No one says anything, at least not to him. But the next day you see a handful of guys wearing loafers or dress shirts, and by the following week it's half the male population of the school. Conforming to nonconformity has become the latest fad.

Into the Word

St. Paul tells Christians to be nonconformists. The pattern of this world is one of evil and corruption, and Christians should not conform to its standards. Instead, Paul says, be transformed—changed—by the renewing of your mind. This transformation doesn't come in an instant; it's a process that goes on over time, and it gives the Christian a new mind—a new way of looking at things and new standards of behavior—as is appropriate for one who, through Baptism, shares in Jesus' death and resurrection.

In My Life

Look at the world around you. Unless you're reading this on a desert island, you will see that the behavior of people around you is basically sinful and selfish. You recognize it as the opposite of what God wants of His people. So you decide, with God's help, not to conform.

Jot down three behaviors you see in the world around you that you do not believe are appropriate for a follower of Jesus.

1. _____

2. _____

3. _____

But changing behaviors isn't the same as being transformed. That's the mistake the Pharisees made. They tried to keep every sentence of the Jewish law without any changes in their sinful, selfish hearts. Jesus called them "white-washed tombs."

Start with the heart. Be transformed by the blood of Jesus which purifies your heart from sin. Ask for the Holy Spirit's help in living a new God-pleasing life according to His standards.

Prayer

Create in me a pure heart, O God, and renew a steadfast spirit within me. Then help me to conform to Your standards. Amen.

Know that the LORD has set apart the godly for Himself; the LORD will hear when I call to Him. *Psalm 4:3*

Something to Think About

We've all had days when we could identify with him—the gangster in the B movie. Gunned down by one of his rivals in a street fight, he lies dying in the arms of the parish priest. "Save your prayers for some goody-goody, Father," he whispers. "After the stuff I've done, the Lord would never listen."

Into the Word

Quite a contrast from King David, isn't it? And he hardly qualified as a goody-goody, either. He'd spent his adult life as a soldier, a leader of troops, planning and carrying out the wholesale murder of his enemies. Then there had been that incident with Bathsheba, when he lusted after another man's wife, gaining her for himself by sending her husband into battle to be killed. His sin led to chaos in his family: His children plotted against each other, and one son, Absalom, attempted to overthrow him.

As David had known sin, he had also known God's forgiveness. He repented of his sin, pleading for God's mercy: "Have mercy on me, O God, according to Your unfailing love; according to Your great compassion blot out my transgressions. Wash away all my iniquity and cleanse me from my sin" (Psalm 51:1–2). Confident of God's forgiveness, David could once again approach God in prayer and praise: "O Lord, open my lips, and my mouth will declare Your praise" (Psalm 51:15). David knew God would listen to his prayers because God had forgiven him and made him His own.

In My Life

You, like David, have been set apart as one of God's own. He has called you by His Gospel, marked you forever with the indelible water of Baptism. He has forgiven your sins through the blood of His Son, Jesus. He sees you as one who has been redeemed, made holy, by His Son.

When you are in trouble—when sin burdens your conscience—He will not turn away and refuse to listen. You belong to Him. He is waiting for your prayer, and He will answer. His answer may not be what you expect or what you want, but it will be the best answer for you.

It's only when you focus on your trouble and your sin that you begin to think that God cannot or will not help. Focus, instead, on God's power and His unfailing love for you.

Prayer

Help me remember, Lord, that I can always come to You because You have made me Your own through Jesus' blood. Amen.

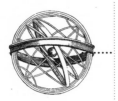

And lead us not into temptation,
but deliver us from the evil one.
Matthew 6:13

Something to Think About

Troy squinted to see through the smokey air in Matt's basement. "Hey, man, glad you're here!" Matt called when he saw Troy. "The beer's in the cooler, and there's plenty of other stuff around. My parents won't be home from Florida 'til next weekend. So hang up your hang-ups, and let's party!"

Matt disappeared into another room with a girl Troy had seen at school. Troy looked around the basement again. There had to be 50 kids just counting those in the rec room—most of them drinking and laughing and having a good time. Troy wondered what Matt's parents would say if they knew about the party.

Troy began to wish he had never come.

Into the Word

"Lead us not into temptation," Matt and Troy had prayed together at church the Sunday before. But here they both were, surrounded. How could God tempt them like this?

Although God sometimes tests His people (remember Abraham and that poor fellow Job?), testing from God is always meant to strengthen faith. The purpose of temptation, on the other hand, is to cause a person to sin. Temptation comes from the devil.

When we pray, "Lead us not into temptation," as Jesus taught us, we ask Him to protect us from the devil and his lies. We know that without His help we will not be able to resist. Like Matt we will give in, willingly following Satan with big grins on our faces. Or like Troy, knowing better, and succumbing anyway.

In My Life

Remember three things when you are tempted. Jesus, your Savior, was tempted just as you are. For 40 days He resisted the devil in the wilderness, never giving in to temptation. His victory over the devil was complete when He died and rose again. And His victory belongs to us too.

Because Jesus has defeated sin and the devil for us, He will stand with us and help us to resist when the devil tempts us. Ask for His help when you are faced with temptation.

And remember, God will not allow the devil to tempt you beyond your endurance. "God is faithful; He will not let you be tempted beyond what you can bear" (1 Corinthians 10:13).

Prayer

Lord Jesus, You defeated the devil for me. Stand by me and help me to resist his temptations today. Amen.

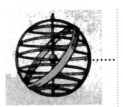

Therefore I tell you, whatever you ask for in prayer, believe that you have received it, and it will be yours. *Mark 11:24*

"Abba, Father," He said, "everything is possible for You. Take this cup from Me. Yet not what I will, but what You will." *Mark 14:36*

Into the Word

Sounds great, doesn't it? Whatever you pray for, you'll get? My prayer list is going to start with this great red sports car and a year's supply of free gas to put in it. It will go on to include the coolest date for this year's prom, a starting position on the basketball team, and straight As to make my parents happy. Are you sure this is true?

Of course, it's true. But you forgot one thing. Most of our prayer lists are motivated by what we want, by what serves our own desires and interests.

Compare that to the way Jesus prayed. He always kept God's interests and desires foremost in His mind. In the Garden of Gethsemane as He bowed under the weight of the sins of all people and faced crucifixion, He prayed, "Take this cup from Me. Yet not what I will, but what You will."

Jesus' prayer was answered in accord with God's will. The following day Jesus died, suffering the punishment that should have fallen on us. It was God's will that we be redeemed, even if it cost Him His only Son.

In My Life

So is it wrong for me to tell God what I want? Doesn't He care that I'm interested in that red sports car?

If God loves you enough to give His Son for you, He cares about everything you're interested in. Tell Him about the sports car, the prom, the basketball team, and the school work too. Psalm 55:22 says, "Cast your cares on the LORD and He will sustain you."

But don't forget Jesus' example. Pray according to God's interests and desires. Accept that He acts in accord with His good and perfect will. Ask Him to ready your heart to rejoice in His will as He works it in your life.

Prayer

Dear Lord, forgive me for selfishly asking You for so many things with nothing but my own interests and desires in mind. Help me to know Your will and to pray according to Your interests and purposes. In the name of Jesus, my Savior. Amen.

The idols of the nations are silver and gold, made by the hands of men. They have mouths, but cannot speak, eyes, but they cannot see; they have ears, but cannot hear, nor is there breath in their mouths. Those who make them will be like them, and so will all who trust in them. *Psalm 135:15–18*

Something to Think About

The ancient Canaanites, neighbors to the Israelites in Old Testament times, worshiped many idols. In addition to Baal and Asherah, the male and female fertility god and goddess, they revered an evil deity named Molech. To appease this angry god, Canaanite parents were required to sacrifice their firstborn children, feeding the god by passing the children into his flaming mouth.

What kind of attitude about the value of human life would you expect to find in people who worshiped a god like Molech?

Into the Word

The writer of Psalm 135 compares the true God to false gods. He recounts the powerful deeds God did in order to bring the Israelites out of slavery in Egypt and lead them to the Promised Land. Idols, on the other hand, have "mouths, but cannot speak, eyes, but they cannot see; ears, but cannot hear" (Psalm 135:16–17); they are powerless. And the people who make them and trust in them are just as powerless.

You can read about a great contest pitting the powers of God against the powers of the idol, Baal, in 1 Kings 18:16–46.

In My Life

What gods do you worship? Not just on Sunday morning, but the rest of the time? What takes priority above everything else in your life? Gods such as money, status, popularity, intellectual achievement, pleasure, or physical fitness don't need faces of silver or gold to rule our lives. Control of our hearts is all that matters.

Be careful—in subtle, imperceptible ways you become like what you worship. And that can be either bad or good news.

It is bad news if you worship a god who makes you think only of yourself and not about the needs and concerns of others. But very good if you worship the true God, who loved even His enemies (that's you and me) so much that He sent His Son to die for them. Being subtly, imperceptibly, more like Him enables us to love and serve one another.

Prayer

God, I have let other concerns become so important that they have become gods in my life. Forgive me, and help me to keep You as my main priority. Amen.

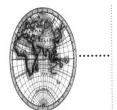

He went to Nazareth, where He had been brought up, and on the Sabbath day He went into the synagogue, as was His custom. *Luke 4:16*

Something to Think About

"I know I should go to church," Rich began, "but I just don't get anything out of it. You know, at our old church in the city the minister really made things relevant to my life. But this preacher out here in Podunkville is dry as dust. Besides, the hymns are slow and boring, and all the members are hypocrites. I can worship better out on the golf course communing with the God of nature."

Into the Word

This one short verse from the gospel of Luke tells us something important about Jesus. On the Sabbath day, the day of worship for the Jews, He went to the synagogue "as was His custom." Jesus was in the habit of public worship. He went to church regularly.

I can't imagine that Jesus, who had been present at the creation of the world and who embodied God's whole plan of salvation, learned a lot from the rabbi in Nazareth. The singing couldn't have compared with the angel choirs in heaven.

And the know-it-all attitude of the other worshipers couldn't have inspired Him: "Isn't this Joseph's Son?" they asked as they drove Him out of town to throw Him down a cliff. Yet Jesus attended synagogue "as was His custom."

In My Life

Not getting much out of church? Here are 10 reasons to go.

1. God commands it: "Remember the Sabbath day ..."
2. You can praise God with other believers for all He has done.
3. You publicly confess your sins and hear the pastor speak words of forgiveness from God.
4. You hear the Scriptures read, explained, and applied to your life.
5. You confess your faith publicly before other believers.
6. You join your prayers with the prayers of other believers.
7. You receive the sacraments in which God touches you physically with His love in church.
8. Your participation supports and encourages the worship of other Christians.
9. The participation of other Christians supports and encourages your worship.
10. Jesus gave us His example to follow. Make church attendance your custom too. For Jesus' sake.

Prayer

Lord, forgive my selfish lack of interest in church and make me look forward to worshiping You with other Christians. Amen.

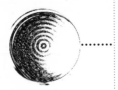

Therefore I glory in Christ Jesus in my service to God. I will not venture to speak of anything except what Christ has accomplished through me in leading the Gentiles to obey God by what I have said and done—by the power of signs and miracles, through the power of the Spirit.
Romans 15:17–19

Into the Word

If anyone had the right to brag, Paul did. He more than any other human being was responsible for bringing the Good News of Christ to the Gentile world. Since his own conversion on the Damascus Road, he had traveled an estimated ten thousand miles preaching the Gospel and establishing a network of churches and Christian communities that provided a solid foundation on which the church would grow. To these churches he penned a series of epistles, explaining doctrine, correcting errors, and exhorting faithfulness in the face of persecution which we can read today in the New Testament.

Along with his teaching and preaching Paul performed signs and miracles through the power of the Spirit. In Lystra he healed a man crippled since birth. He cast an evil spirit out of a slave girl in Philippi. He brought Eutychus back to life after he had fallen to his death.

But listen to Paul's boast: "I will not venture to speak of anything except what Christ has accomplished through me in leading the Gentiles to obey God" (Romans 15:18). Not Paul, but Jesus Christ, and Jesus working through Paul, His instrument. In his letters to the Corinthians he quoted the psalmist: "Let him who boasts boast in the Lord" (1 Corinthians 1:31, 2 Corinthians 10:17).

Paul knew the difference between improper and proper boasting. He knew that all he had accomplished could never make him right with God: "For it is by grace you have been saved, through faith—and this not from yourselves, it is the gift of God—not by works, so that no one can boast," he wrote (Ephesians 2:8–9). Instead he boasted in the crucified Christ: "May I never boast except in the cross of our Lord Jesus Christ, through which the world has been crucified to me, and I to the world" (Galatians 6:14).

In My Life

So go ahead and boast. Tell everyone what Christ has done for you and through you. It's another way of praising your Lord.

Prayer

Till then—nor is my boasting vain—
Till then I boast a Savior slain;
And oh, may this my glory be,
That Christ is not ashamed of me! Amen.

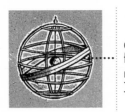

For all have sinned and fall short of the glory of God, and are justified freely by His grace through the redemption that came by Christ Jesus. *Romans 3:23–24*

Something to Think About

"How do you think you did on the biology test, Jeff?" asked Molly.

"Well, I know I missed the questions on cell division, and I might have mixed up a couple on genes and chromosomes, but other than that, I think I got them all right. That should give me an A, or at least a B+ because I think most of the other guys missed a lot more than that. Mrs. Wiley always grades on the curve."

That good old grading curve has saved a lot of us who would have failed if the teacher had used an absolute grading scale in which the grade is determined by the number of mistakes you made.

Which grading scale does God use?

Into the Word

Many people believe God grades on the curve. "Sure, I've made some mistakes," they say, "but I've led a much better life than most people. I go to church more often than average, and I don't drink or smoke as much as my friends. I'll probably get to go to heaven."

But Paul tells us in Romans that God's scale is absolute. "The wages of sin is death" (Romans 6:23), he writes. What a tough scale—one mistake, and you fail! And no one can get a perfect score—"For all have sinned and fall short of the glory of God" (Romans 3:23).

But God loved us so much He sent His Son to take our place. Our sins were placed on Him, and He was nailed to the cross. His righteousness was placed on us so that we stand before God without sin. God looks at us, sees Jesus' righteousness, and records a perfect score: "... justified freely by His grace through the redemption that came by Christ Jesus" (Romans 3:24).

In My Life

What does God's grace in Jesus mean to us? It means we no longer have to worry about not being good enough on God's grading scale. Freed from sin, we can live the way God intended us to live: praising Him as our Redeemer, telling everyone what He has done for us, and serving other people in love.

Prayer

Lord, I know I fall short of Your absolute standard. But I believe that, by Your grace, You sent Jesus to die to pay for my sin. Forgive me for His sake, and help me to live for You. Amen.

Now when a man works, his wages are not credited to him as a gift, but as an obligation. However, to the man who does not work but trusts God who justifies the wicked, his faith is credited as righteousness. *Romans 4:4-5*

Something to Think About

The great reformer, Martin Luther, was desperate. As a monk in the Augustinian Cloister at Erfurt, Germany, he followed the requirements of his order to the letter: hourly prayer, menial tasks around the cloister, studying the writings of the church fathers, and begging for alms. Yet he was tormented by the worry that he hadn't done enough to appease an angry God. He said of himself, "It is true, I was a pious monk. I kept my vows so conscientiously that I am sure if ever a monk had gotten to heaven through his monkery, I should have gotten there. If I had continued longer, I would have tortured myself to death with prayer, fasting, waking, and freezing. Yet I was in such despair that I thought God was not gracious to me" (From *The Church Throughout the Ages*, S. J. Roth and Wm. A. Kramer. St. Louis: Concordia Publishing House, 1949, 1957 edition: 352).

Into the Word

In his study of the Bible Luther was led to Paul's epistle to the Romans. In this letter Paul, inspired by the Holy Spirit, explains to the Roman Christians that being justified before God doesn't depend on anything we do. Our salvation is entirely a gift from God which we receive through faith.

Paul explains that wages aren't a gift at all; they're the reward that's owed us for work we have done. But grace is different. "This righteousness from God comes through faith in Jesus Christ to all who believe" (Romans 3:22), Paul writes, whether they lived as model Christians or as criminals, "for all have sinned and fall short of the glory of God, and are justified freely by His grace through the redemption that came by Christ Jesus" (Romans 3:23).

In My Life

Faith is the key. But how can you be sure you have enough faith?

Faith isn't something we do; it's a gift from God. "For it is by grace you have been saved, through faith—and this not from yourselves, it is the gift of God—not by works, so that no one can boast" (Ephesians 2:8–9). We can't make it start or grow—that's the Holy Spirit's doing. And even the tiniest faith—no larger than a mustard seed, Jesus said—can hold on to the grace of God in Jesus Christ.

Prayer

Amazing grace! How sweet the sound
That saved a wretch like me!
I once was lost but now am found,
Was blind but now I see. Amen.

Now Thomas (called Didymus), one of the Twelve, was not with the disciples when Jesus came. So the other disciples told him, "We have seen the Lord!"

But he said to them, "Unless I see the nail marks in His hands and put my finger where the nails were, and put my hand into His side, I will not believe it."

Then Jesus told him, "Because you have seen Me, you have believed; blessed are those who have not seen and yet have believed." *John 20:24–25, 29*

Something to Think About

In high school physics when you study about electricity, you learn that an electric current flows when an electron, the tiniest part of the atom, moves from the outermost shell of one atom to the outermost shell of another atom to replace an electron that has moved from that atom to another.

Although the physics book says this is true, you have never seen any of these minuscule particles. To accept this theory of electricity, you must believe in the existence of atoms. You must believe that each atom has a small nucleus orbited by an even smaller electron. And then you must believe in the ordered movement of these electrons to produce current. You have never seen any of this. But that doesn't stop you from turning on the kitchen light switch, watching television, or listening to the stereo. Although you can't see electricity, you experience its power hundreds of times each day.

Into the Word

Thomas, the modern disciple with the skeptical mind, wanted to see the risen Christ before he believed. Jesus showed him, and Thomas confessed his faith.

But faith is more than seeing. "Faith is being sure of what we hope for and certain of what we do not see" (Hebrews 11:1). For postascension Christians like us, Jesus' words hold special assurance: "Blessed are those who have not seen and yet have believed" (John 20:29).

Because we have not physically seen Jesus, we value the picture of Him that we have through His inspired Word. And we never let the fact that we have not seen Him keep us from experiencing His power within us through faith.

Prayer

Lord, through Your Holy Spirit help me to believe in You whom I have not seen. Reassure me through Your Word of Your love and forgiveness, until I see You with my own eyes in heaven. Amen.

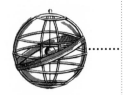

Set a guard over my mouth, O LORD; keep watch over the door of my lips. Let not my heart be drawn to what is evil, to take part in wicked deeds with men who are evildoers. *Psalm 141:3–4a*

Something to Think About

When I was a child, my mother kept a bar of laundry soap on the counter next to the kitchen sink. Because I had a problem with my mouth, I lived in dread of that bar of soap. Telling lies meant getting my mouth washed out with soap. Swearing resulted in an oral sudsing, as did using "bathroom words" for anything other than bathroom needs. Sometimes even "sassing" or talking back brought out the soap.

I'm not sure if I learned to control my mouth or to hate the taste of soap bubbles. Soap that worked on the heart would have been a more effective remedy.

Into the Word

The writer of Psalm 141 recognized the trouble a mouth can cause. So did the apostle James: "The tongue is a small part of the body, but it makes great boasts. ... The tongue also is a fire, a world of evil among the parts of the body. It corrupts the whole person, sets the whole course of his life on fire, and is itself set on fire by hell" (James 3:5–6).

But Jesus pinpointed the source of the mouth's problem. "But the things that come out of the mouth come from the heart, and these make a man 'unclean.' For out of the heart come evil thoughts, murder, adultery, sexual immorality, theft, false testimony, slander" (Matthew 15:18–19).

In My Life

Do you have mouth trouble? Or, does your problem really come from your heart?

The Word of God gives the perfect remedy for a heart soiled by sin. "Cleanse me with hyssop, and I will be clean; wash me, and I will be whiter than snow. Create in me a pure heart, O God, and renew a steadfast spirit within me" (Psalm 51:7, 10). The soap? "The blood of Jesus, His Son, purifies us from all sin" (1 John 1:7).

So get to the source of "mouth" trouble—ask God to clean your heart from sin by the blood of His Son, Jesus. Cleansed by Jesus' blood, the words of your mouth, as well as the thoughts of your heart, will be acceptable in the sight of God.

Prayer

Lord, my words come from the sinful thoughts of my heart. Purify my heart with Your forgiveness, won by the blood of Jesus, my Savior. Then let my words bring the love, hope, and comfort to others that Your words bring to me. Amen.

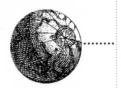

Woe to the world because of the things that cause people to sin! Such things must come, but woe to the man through whom they come!
Matthew 18:7

Something to Think About

Brad could hardly wait for Friday night to come. Jeff had invited everyone who was anybody to his graduation party—the whole football team, the cheerleaders, the group from the ski club. Although Brad was only a sophomore, he knew a lot of the kids from student council and pep club, but he couldn't believe Jeff had included him.

On Tuesday before the party Jeff stopped Brad in the hall. "By the way, Brad," he said casually, "just figure on staying overnight Friday at my house. My mom and dad said if anybody gets in trouble on the way home from the party, they'd be responsible since they're buying the beer. My mom says you all better sleep on the floor and go home in the morning."

"Sure, no problem," mumbled Brad as Jeff walked over to talk to another group of kids. But after Jeff left, Brad stood and thought for a long time about what to do.

Into the Word

Temptation. It's not a sin, but it's always

trying to lead you there. "Try it—you'll like it!" "It can't be wrong if it feels good." "Everybody's doing it!" "You have to look out for number one."

If it's any consolation, you're not alone. Everyone who has ever lived has had to deal with temptation—even Jesus! To learn how the devil tempted Him and how He handled it, read Matthew 4:1–11. And temptation always follows the same old patterns. Paul wrote, "No temptation has seized you except what is common to man" (1 Corinthians 10:13a).

Paul also provides the way out. "God is faithful," Paul promises; "He will not let you be tempted beyond what you can bear. But when you are tempted, He will also provide a way out so that you can stand up under it" (1 Corinthians 10:13b).

In My Life

The next time you are tempted, look for the way out. Close the textbook left open during the exam. Don't bring your date home when your parents are gone. Stay home from the party where you know alcohol and drugs will be available. The same Jesus who died to forgive your sins will help you resist the temptation to keep on sinning.

Prayer Thought

When you go to Jesus for forgiveness, ask Him to help you find a way out of temptation.

Then everyone deserted Him and fled. *Mark 14:50*

Into the Word

Doesn't it make you furious? When you read the story of Jesus' suffering and death, don't you wonder how the characters in the story could have been so cruel? Even if they didn't understand who He really was, they certainly could see that He wasn't guilty of a crime deserving of death. And how could they have been so blind about His identity after all the miracles they had seen?

Pontius Pilate, for example, came right out and admitted he knew Jesus was innocent. Because of his fear of the Jews and his Roman superiors, he condemned this innocent Man to death. How could he?

And the Sanhedrin, the ruling religious council of the Jews, met at night, against their own regulations, to hear the words of false witnesses who contradicted each other. They ridiculed and abused Jesus and demanded Pilate put Him to death. How could they?

We would never have caused our Lord the pain these sinners caused. We would have been more like His disciples. Well, maybe not like Judas who betrayed the Master he had followed for three years. And not like Peter who denied knowing Him for the privilege of standing near a fire. How could they have treated their best Friend so badly?

We would not treat Him like that. We would not be like the others. "Everyone deserted Him and fled" (Mark 14:50). Thomas, Matthew, Andrew, Philip, and the rest. They too added to His pain in His hour of death by running away in terror. How could they?

In My Life

It's easy, isn't it, to point to murderers and rapists, con men and terrorists, and feel good about our own behavior by comparison. But according to God's standards, we are all guilty of sin and deserve to die. The disciples were no better than the Sanhedrin; you and I fare the same as the criminals. "There is no difference, for all have sinned and fall short of the glory of God" (Romans 3:22–23).

Me, a sinner? Guilty as charged and responsible for Christ's death. And that leads directly to the good news—"But God demonstrates His own love for us in this: While we were still sinners, Christ died for us" (Romans 5:8). The sins Jesus carried to the cross were ours. The victory over sin and death He won is ours too.

Prayer

Lord Jesus, I confess all my sins to You. Forgive them through Your holy, precious blood that You shed for me. Amen.

When the devil had finished all this tempting, he left Him until an opportune time. *Luke 4:13*

Something to Think About

Can you remember a time when you, with God's help, were able to resist temptation?

Talk with a parent or a Christian friend about temptation. Ask them to tell you about a temptation that they faced and resisted. How did God help them to keep from giving in? Share your temptation story with your parent or friend.

You may feel a real sense of accomplishment in standing firm in the face of temptation. You may even say, "I made it with God's help! Now that's the end of that." Right?

Wrong!

Into the Word

After Jesus was baptized by John, at the beginning of His earthly ministry, He went into the wilderness for 40 days and nights. Here the devil tempted Him: "If You're the Son of God, tell this stone to become bread"; "I will give You all the authority and splendor of the kingdoms of this world if You worship me"; "If You are the Son of God, throw Yourself down from the highest point of the temple."

Jesus countered each temptation with God's Word. "It is written: 'Man does not live by bread alone.' " "It is written: 'Worship the Lord your God and serve Him only.' " "It says: 'Do not put the Lord your God to the test.' "

For the only time in the history of the world, a Man had resisted all of the devil's temptations. Jesus had won. One would think the devil would have slunk back to hell and never bothered Him again. But he didn't. He just waited for a more opportune time.

He was there on the hillside where Jesus fed the 5,000 who wanted to make Him King. There in the garden when Jesus could have avoided the suffering of His Father's will. There on Calvary in the taunts of the crowd to come down and save Himself. Each time Jesus resisted. And Jesus won.

In My Life

As the devil continued to tempt Jesus, so he continues to tempt you. But through His death and resurrection Jesus sealed the devil's ultimate defeat. He gives you the power to resist the devil's assaults, using the same weapon He used—God's Word.

Prayer

Lord Jesus, You defeated the devil for me. Help me to resist his temptations, knowing my final victory is already decided because I belong to You. Amen.

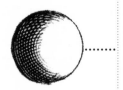

Have mercy on me, O God, according to Your unfailing love; according to Your great compassion blot out my transgressions. Wash away all my iniquity and cleanse me from my sin.
Psalm 51:1–2

Something to Think About

Kristy hugged her mother tightly. The evening had drained them both emotionally. First the confrontation when Officer Simpson brought Kristy home and told her mom she had been caught shoplifting. Then the angry words, the tears, the apologies, and the promises never to do it again. Finally, her mom's forgiveness and going to God together in prayer to ask for His forgiveness too.

"Thanks, Mom," said Kristy with a smile of relief. "I think I'll go to the mall with Karen for a couple hours before it closes. See you later."

"Hold on a minute, young lady," her mom interrupted. "You're grounded for the next four weeks until you finish those young offenders classes at Juvenile Court."

Kristy couldn't believe her ears. She thought her mom had forgiven her.

Into the Word

When David wrote the words of Psalm 51, he probably felt a lot like Kristy. He had committed adultery with Bathsheba, the wife of one of his officers, and now Bathsheba was pregnant. So David sent the officer into the front lines of battle where he would be killed. God's prophet, Nathan, confronted David with his sin, and David repented and asked for God's forgiveness. God heard David's prayer and forgave his sin.

If this were a fairy tale, everyone would live happily ever after. But this story is real, and in real life even forgiven people must live with the consequences of their sin. David's baby son died. For the rest of his life David was plagued by family problems that stemmed from his sin.

In My Life

When you confess your sin to God, you can trust completely in His promise to forgive you. Jesus has already taken the punishment for your sin.

But be prepared to live with sin's consequences. When you violate the trust of your parents, teachers, or friends, they will not be so quick to trust you again. When you break the law, you will face the consequences the law prescribes. When you treat your friends badly, they will find other friends.

Prayer

Lord, forgive me for what I have done wrong. Please help other people to forgive me too. Then give me the strength and maturity to live with the consequences of my sin and to restore the relationships I have broken. In Jesus' name. Amen.

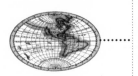

How can a young man keep his way pure? By living according to Your word. I seek You with all my heart; do not let me stray from Your commands. I have hidden Your word in my heart that I might not sin against You. *Psalm 119:9–11*

Something to Think About

Young men and women who are trying to set standards for their lives often look to the quotations of famous individuals for guidance. By following the philosophy exhibited in the quotation, the young person may establish the direction in which he wants his life to proceed.

For example, the individual who chooses Nathan Hale's "I only regret that I have but one life to lose for my country" will live differently and pursue different goals from the person who chooses P. T. Barnum's "There's a sucker born every minute."

Ask your parent and another adult you admire what quotation they feel best represents their lives.

Into the Word

If you asked the psalmist for his meaningful quotation, he would definitely quote the Word of God. He has studied it, memorized it, and taken it to heart: "I have hidden Your word in my heart that I might not sin against You" (Psalm 119:11). His knowledge of and love for God's Word determines the way he lives; it keeps him from sin.

In My Life

What does God's Word have to say to you to determine the course of your life? Perhaps one of these quotations, perhaps another.

To keep your priorities straight and live in a God-pleasing way: "Love the Lord your God with all your heart and with all your soul and with all your mind. Love your neighbor as yourself" (Matthew 22:37, 39).

When none of your plans seem to be working out: "And we know that in all things God works for the good of those who love Him, who have been called according to His purpose" (Romans 8:28).

When you're worried about the future: "For I am convinced that neither death nor life, neither angels nor demons, neither the present nor the future, nor any powers, neither height nor depth, nor anything else in all creation, will be able to separate us from the love of God that is in Christ Jesus our Lord" (Romans 8:38–39).

Prayer

O Lord, hide Your word in my heart to give direction to my life and to keep me from sin. When I fail, forgive me for the sake of Your Son, Jesus. Amen.

Wanting to satisfy the crowd, Pilate released Barabbas to them. He had Jesus flogged, and handed Him over to be crucified. *Mark 15:15*

Something to Think About

Scott hesitated by the candy at the end of the closed checkout lane. Of course he had been taught never to steal. But this was different. The rest of the guys had already left the store with their pockets full of candy bars. If he showed up empty handed, they would think he was a coward. He'd be all alone again, with no friends, and who knows how much trouble he'd get into then.

Tracy hadn't slept all week, but at least she had finally come to a decision. Her parents would be devastated if they knew about her pregnancy. They would be too embarrassed to face their friends once everyone found out—especially the ladies from Mom's Right to Life group. Andy had found a safe abortion clinic and borrowed enough money to pay the fees. Of course she had always thought abortion was wrong. She was only doing this for her parents.

Situational ethics—it's when our concept of right and wrong depends on the situation we're in.

Into the Word

Pontius Pilate was an expert at rationalization. He knew Jesus wasn't guilty. But the Jewish mob was angry, and the religious leaders had made their threats: "If you let this man go, you are no friend of Caesar" (John 19:12). His attempts to get them to compromise on releasing Jesus instead of Barabbas had failed. "Surely any governor would be satisfied to avert mob violence, even if it meant executing one innocent Man," Pilate must have reasoned. "Whose life is more important, anyway—this backwater Rabbi's or mine?"

In My Life

God has given us very clear statements of right and wrong. "Love the Lord, your God," He demands, by making Him first in every part of your life, by respecting and honoring His holy name, and by worshiping Him. "Love your neighbor as yourself" by obeying and respecting parents and others in authority, preserving human life in all its forms, honoring human sexuality and the family as gifts from God, helping others to keep what belongs to them, speaking the truth in love, and being content with what God has given you.

We haven't met God's standards for living; we have often compromised to keep ourselves and others happy. But through Jesus, God forgives our sins and gives us eternal life.

Prayer

Forgive me, Lord, for Jesus' sake, for compromising Your rules for the situations in which I find myself. Forgiven, help me to live according to Your standards. Amen.

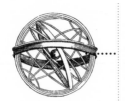

So Joseph bought some linen cloth, took down the body, wrapped it in the linen, and placed it in a tomb cut out of rock. Then he rolled a stone against the entrance of the tomb. Mary Magdalene and Mary the mother of Joses saw where He was laid. *Mark 15:46–47*

Something to Think About

What epitaph would you like to see on your tombstone at the end of your life? One Christian mother who raised a family and kept a home, taught Sunday school and sang in the choir, baked pies for church socials, made evangelism calls, and visited the elderly in nursing homes chose these words: She did what she could.

Into the Word

First-century Jewish law and custom was more concerned with what women couldn't do than with what they could. The women who followed Jesus were legally barred from testifying in a court of law in His behalf. They were not allowed to appeal to Pontius Pilate. They couldn't persuade the Jewish mob to stop its madness or overpower the Roman soldiers on the crucifixion detail.

But the women did what they could. When the disciples fled in fear, the women stood watch until their Master died. They helped Joseph wrap the body in linen and lay it in the tomb. They mentally marked the tomb's location and returned early Sunday morning to anoint their Lord's body with spices.

God rewarded their simple, faithful service. They, not the disciples, were the first to find the empty tomb and hear the angel's message: "He has risen! He is not here" (Mark 16:6).

After Jesus' ascension they waited with the disciples in Jerusalem for the coming of the Holy Spirit. And they played important roles in the Christian church in the exciting days following Pentecost.

In My Life

What's keeping you from serving Jesus? Are you too young to organize a missionary expedition? Not allowed to preach because of your gender? Too broke to finance an educational wing for your church? Not educated enough to write a treatise on theology?

Instead of focusing on what you can't do, do what you can. Love a child who needs a friend. Visit with someone who's lonely. Tell someone about the joy of knowing Jesus as your Savior. Offer to help with vacation Bible school, or trim the grass and plant flowers on the church property. Pray for your pastor and the members of your church. God will bless your efforts, just as He did those of the women who followed Jesus.

Prayer Thought

Ask God to help you find ways to serve Him and others to show your joy for all Jesus has done for you.